# SURROGACY LAW

## IN A NUTSHELL®

JOSEPH F. MORRISSEY
Professor of Law
Stetson University College of Law

WEST ACADEMIC

860 Blue Gentian Road, Suite 350
Eagan, MN 55121
1-877-888-1330



Published in the United States of America

**ISBN:** 979-8-89209-742-0

# ACKNOWLEDGMENTS

This book is dedicated to my family: my husband, Mark Montgomery, and our two amazing children, Sam and Frank, who are the miraculous result of our surrogacy journey.

I am also thankful to Stetson University College of Law for honoring me with the Leroy Highbaugh Sr. Chair, which provided me with support to undertake and complete this book. Finally, this book would never have been possible without the editorial and research support of my friends and colleagues Janice Strawn, Johnathan Urquhart, and Brendan Lee.

# OUTLINE

# TABLE OF CASES

**References are to Pages**

# SURROGACY LAW
# IN A NUTSHELL®

# INTRODUCTION

**Surrogacy is transformative.** Surrogacy involves a gestational carrier, a surrogate, carrying one or more babies for another person or a couple who are the intended parent or parents. I wrote this book because surrogacy changed our lives forever. My husband and I became the parents of two beautiful twin boys with the help of a wonderful woman who was our surrogate. We will be forever indebted to her. We were also assisted by incredibly supportive professionals who helped us navigate our way through the process. Now, many years later, we are consumed with homework, play dates, soccer practices, and spelling bees. We are generally exhausted, but are also profoundly fulfilled by our family life. As such, we know that surrogacy can help people achieve their dream of building a family.

**Surrogacy is exploding in popularity.** Surrogacy has made parents out of people who thought it might never be possible. Because of its growing popularity, surrogacy is also the current focus of much media attention. People Magazine, for example, regularly reports on celebrities who have pursued family formation through the use of surrogacy, including Anderson Cooper, Rebel Wilson, Alec and Hilaria Baldwin, Kristen Wiig and Avi Rothman, Priyanka Chopra and Nick Jonas, Matthew Broderick and Sarah Jessica Parker, Neil

Patrick Harris and David Burtka, and so many others.[1]

But surrogacy, of course, isn't just for the rich and famous. More and more intended parents generally are turning to surrogacy for family formation. While precise numbers are difficult to ascertain, the Centers for Disease Control (CDC) does publish statistics about the use of assisted reproductive technologies (ART) in the United States. The CDC reports that in 2012 there were 3,202 embryo transfers using a gestational surrogate. By 2019, that number reached a high of 9,195; and in 2021 the number had come down a bit to 8,862.[2]

**Surrogacy involves a wide array of people who make family formation possible.** Intended parents have different reasons for pursuing surrogacy. For us, as a gay couple seeking to start a family, our choices were to foster, adopt, or pursue surrogacy. When we were contemplating starting a family, adoption was categorically illegal for gay people in Florida where we were living at the time.[3]

---

[1] Jen Juneau, *Famous Families Who've Welcomed Children Through Surrogacy,* PEOPLE, (Jan. 25, 2023, 3:50 PM) https://people.com/parents/celebrities-who-have-used-surrogates/.

[2] CTRS. FOR DISEASE CONTROL AND PREVENTION, 2019 ASSISTED REPRODUCTIVE TECHNOLOGY FERTILITY CLINIC AND NATIONAL SUMMARY REPORT 34 (2019), https://archive.cdc.gov/#/details?url=https://www.cdc.gov/art/reports/2019/pdf/2019-Report-ART-Fertility-Clinic-National-Summary-h.pdf.

[3] The ban on adoption by gay people in Florida read, "No person eligible to adopt . . . may adopt if that person is a homosexual." FLA. STAT. ANN. § 63.042(3) (West 2014). That ban was first ruled unconstitutional in the 2010 case of Fla. Dep't of Child. & Fams. v. *In re* Adoption of X.X.G., 45 So. 3d 79, 92 (Fla.

We could have become foster parents, but didn't like the potential impermanence of that. We could have moved and adopted in a different state. But that was going to be personally and professionally extremely difficult. We also liked the idea of being genetically related to our children. So, we chose surrogacy. For traditional couples, or single women, surrogacy often makes sense when the intended mother has medical risks or difficulties associated with carrying a child. For single gay men, surrogacy is a great way to have genetically related children.

Surrogates themselves are at the center of the process. Surrogates choose to become involved for a wide array of reasons. Our surrogate, a doula, was uniquely interested in maternity generally and in helping people in need form their families. She had a child of her own and had been a surrogate once before, but was ready to help another family when she was introduced to us. For other surrogates, the compensation drives the decision, and can help the surrogate pursue her own dreams while she helps intended parents form their family.

Egg donors are sometimes a part of the process. For us, as gay men, that was the case. Others who have fertility issues may need the help of an egg donor as well. In some cases, the intended parent or parents may need the help of a sperm donor. Egg or sperm donors are sometimes family members who are happy to help their relatives achieve their family formation goals. Having a relative be the biological

---

Dist. Ct. App. 2010); and finally officially repealed by statute in 2015. 2015 Fla. Sess. Law Serv. Ch. 2015–130 (West).

parent of your child has its own dynamics. Some people may be touched by that connectivity, but others would prefer not to have that potential complication where the biological parent may later seek to be overly involved in the child's upbringing. In many cases, therefore, the donors are anonymous and are paid for their contribution.

In many cases, intended parents need the additional help of an agency, a fertility clinic, a family law attorney, or another professional to pursue surrogacy. Intended parents, surrogates and egg or sperm donors often find each other through surrogacy agencies or fertility clinics. The costs of working through an agency can be quite high, with the intended parents generally bearing the expenses. But agencies and clinics give intended parents options and support. They help intended parents match with appropriate surrogates and donors, and help all the parties navigate the process safely and legally. Attorneys are crucial too, as they will help all the parties understand and navigate the risks associated with the procedures and process. Those risks are generally discussed and arrangements are agreed upon in appropriate contracts between the parties.

**Surrogacy allows intended parents to build families by agreement.** Surrogacy can be expensive and complicated, but with the right amount of desire and a little guidance, the process can be managed and understood. Surrogacy is based on an array of carefully thought through contracts. For every party that is involved in the surrogacy arrangement, there is typically an agreement between that party and the intended parent or parents. However, the contracts do more than create legally binding sets of reciprocal expectations. The contracts also help the parties involved methodically think through, in advance, the issues that can arise in connection with egg donation and surrogacy.

Typically, each party to any of the contracts involved in surrogacy is represented by an attorney. The costs here generally fall on the intended parent or parents, who typically pay for separate and independent attorneys to assist the surrogate and/or any egg or sperm donor.

The attorneys will lead the parties through the issues involved in their related contract. After thorough soul searching and guided discussion of the issues road mapped in the contract, the parties may decide that they should not work together. Sometimes that is the best decision. However, if, with the help of the attorneys, the parties do agree on how the process should unfold, and how to manage unexpected developments, then having had those discussions in advance can assure a smoother process going forward.

So, for an easy example, intended parents and their surrogates should discuss the possibility of the surrogate getting pregnant with more than one embryo. What does that mean for the arrangement? Typically, the surrogate will receive extra compensation to account for the increased difficulty of carrying multiples. However, more dire circumstances also need to be addressed. All the parties need to contemplate what would happen, for example, if the pregnancy becomes life threatening for the surrogate. Would all the parties agree to terminate the pregnancy? These difficult questions may not be thought about in advance but for the roadmap of a surrogacy agreement that should cover the wide array of potential developments.

Those discussions help the parties discover whether they truly should pursue surrogacy, and whether the particular counterparty they have found is the right fit for them for their surrogacy experience. For the surrogate, she can assess whether the particular intended parents she is beginning to work with are compatible with her approach to the issues involved, or whether she may want to wait and find a different set of intended parents who share more similar values and attitudes. For the intended parents, they can assess whether they are comfortable with the surrogate and her approach to thinking about all of the potentialities. Even if common values are shared between the parties, and the parties are able to agree on how to approach various potential developments, personality differences might become apparent in the discussions that make one or the other party uncomfortable working with the counterparty.

Those intangible feelings are crucial and can be discovered through the process of discussing the surrogacy arrangement in advance. Our surrogate was clear with us that she only wanted to give the gift of her being a surrogate to a couple who she really liked, and thought were solid as a couple, and would make great parents. I am pretty sure that when we met our surrogate, she had a healthy skepticism about whether she wanted to work with us, but eventually decided we were the right fit. And she was right, we have had a terrific relationship with her both during her surrogacy of our twin boys and now many years later.

As with so many decisions in life, sometimes a decision not to move forward can be the best decision. But, for surrogates and intended parents who find common ground through the planning discussions and who appreciate the approach, personalities, and demeanor of the other parties, the surrogacy relationship is much more likely to be successful.

**The legal infrastructure for surrogacy is complex and varied.** Underlying all of the agreements involved in a surrogacy arrangement is the legal infrastructure in each state in the United States that may or may not enforce a surrogacy arrangement. There has been a strong trend over the past decades for states to embrace and support surrogacy. Now, surrogacy is permitted in the vast majority of the states. However, **surrogacy agreements are not enforceable in every state** in the United States and surrogacy agreements for compensation are still even punishable criminally in Michigan.[4]

For some states, surrogacy may be permissible because it is simply not prohibited by any statute or

---

[4] Surrogate Parenting Act, MICH. COMP. LAWS ANN. § 722.851–63 (West 2023).

by caselaw. But in many states there are specific enabling statutes that authorize and regulate surrogacy. It is crucial that the parties seeking a surrogacy arrangement make sure they do so in a jurisdiction that enforces such arrangements. You can be more confident of that in jurisdictions that have enacted statutes to allow and regulate surrogacy. If not, then, at a minimum, parties should engage in a surrogacy arrangement with the clear understanding of the risk that their arrangement might not be enforceable if any party decides not to follow through with their promises.

For example, for us, residents of Florida at the time, the law provided and still provides that surrogacy contracts are only enforceable when the intended parents are a married couple and the "commissioning mother" has medical issues that would prevent her from carrying a healthy fetus to term.[5] Well, at the time we were entering into our contract, back in 2013, it was not legal for us to be married in Florida, and we didn't have a "commissioning mother." So, our surrogacy agreement would not likely have been upheld in the state of Florida.

Even though I am a law professor and teach Contract Law, we had enlisted the help of an attorney who was very experienced with surrogacy arrangements. She had advised that we make the contract subject to the laws of a different state, one which provided for the enforceability of our

---

[5] FLA. STAT. ANN. § 742.15 (West 2023).

agreement and one with which we had reasonable connections to make the choice of a law outside of Florida reasonable. We chose to have the laws of Illinois, a state with a very supportive surrogacy law, govern our agreement. We had started our surrogacy journey with a surrogacy agency based in Chicago. We were both originally from Illinois, and we spent summers in Illinois where we owned property. So, we were optimistic that our choice of Illinois law would be upheld if challenged, and so would our agreement. Thankfully, our agreement was never subject to any disputes, and we never had to definitively find out.

**Surrogacy involves professionals and academics.** This book is not only for potential intended parents, surrogates, and donors, but also for professionals and academics focusing on surrogacy. The book provides an overview of the process and the potential issues that can arise for the parties involved. The professionals will hopefully appreciate the detail set forth about the legal risks involved that need to be managed and the contracts involved that need to be structured to minimize that risk.

Beyond contract law, constitutional law is also implicated in different and perhaps some surprising ways. First, there is an argument that state laws prohibiting surrogacy and thus limiting the ability of individuals to form families could (and perhaps should) be deemed unconstitutional. The ability of an individual to have natural children and raise them the way the individual sees fit has repeatedly been said by the federal courts to be a fundamental constitutional right.[6]

Second, IVF itself has come under fire in the United States in the recent past. In *Dobbs v. Jackson Women's Health Organization* in 2022 the United States Supreme Court overturned a woman's constitutional right to choose to have an abortion.[7] In the wake of *Dobbs*, in February of 2024, the State Supreme Court of Alabama ruled in *LePage v. Center for Reproductive Medicine* that embryos created through IVF are "unborn children" and thus the state's wrongful death statute could be applied when and if the embryos are destroyed.[8] That opinion was widely criticized and a statute was quickly passed in Alabama to immunize IVF clinics from potential wrongful death liability.[9] Nonetheless, the issue remains of whether IVF may come under further pressure, particularly in more conservative states. If so, surrogacy arrangements, which necessarily involve IVF, would be at risk in those states.

---

6 Going back 100 years, the U.S. Supreme Court held that parents have a liberty interest under the 14th Amendment of the Constitution "to marry, establish a home, and bring up children." Meyer v. Nebraska, 262 U.S. 390, 399 (1923). That case involved a prohibition on teaching German to school children.

7 Dobbs v. Jackson Women's Health Organization, 597 U.S. 215 (2022).

8 LePage v. Center for Reproductive Medicine, P.C. No. SC-2022-0515 (Sup. Ct. Al, 2024).

9 Azeen Ghorayshi and Sarah Kliff, *IVF Threats in Alabama Drive Clinics to Ship Out Embryos*, N.Y. TIMES (Aug. 12, 2024), https://www.nytimes.com/2024/08/12/health/ivf-embryos-alabama.html?smid=em-share.

Constitutional law is implicated again, however, in an equal rights context. In our situation, we found that the federal government, which had allowed tax deductions for medical expenses related to surrogacy, did not allow those deductions for us. The federal district court ruled that because we, as gay men, were not technically infertile, we didn't have a medical necessity that needed treatment and thus could not deduct our sizeable expenses.[10] We actually challenged that ruling and brought suit in federal court, taking it up to the federal court of appeals for the 11th Circuit (of which Florida is a part). Unfortunately, we lost, but still believe strongly that our treatment was both unreasonable and unconstitutional.

This book builds from our personal experience with surrogacy as intended parents, but also from my background as a law professor who teaches both Contract and Constitutional Law, and has authored a casebook in the field of contracts. It is designed to help the parties involved in surrogacy understand the complex array of issues that are implicated in each type of agreement and the surrogacy arrangement overall. It is my hope that this book will inspire those contemplating surrogacy to pursue their dream and also give some guidance to professionals and academics to help those people achieve miraculous results.

---

[10] Morrissey v. United States, 226 F.Supp. 3d 1338, 1344 (M.D. Fla. 2016), *aff'd*, 871 F.3d 1260 (11th Cir. 2017).

# CHAPTER 1

# OUR SURROGACY STORY

Our personal story about surrogacy begins when my husband, Mark, and I met in 2000. In the early years we were together, we never really considered marriage or children. We had grown up in a country and in communities where gay marriage was illegal, and gay people having children was usually the product of an earlier opposite-sex marriage. As our relationship evolved, however, so did the country's attitudes toward same-sex relationships, marriage, and families.

In 2003, Massachusetts became the first state to legalize gay marriage.[1] Other states followed.[2] Everything seemed to be in flux. Some states had legalized gay marriage only to take a turnabout and prohibit them again. In California, gay couples who had married when it was legal continued to have their marriage respected even though new gay marriages were later prohibited.[3] The issue of gay

---

[1] Goodridge v. Dep't of Pub. Health, 798 N.E.2d 941, 969–70 (Mass. 2003).

[2] For example, in 2008 Connecticut was the second state to legalize gay marriage. *See* Kerrigan v. Comm'r of Pub. Health, 957 A.2d 407, 482 (Conn. 2008). Iowa followed in 2009. *See* Varnum v. Brien, 763 N.W.2d 862, 907 (Iowa 2009).

[3] In 2008, a statutory ban on gay marriage was ruled unconstitutional in California under the California constitution. *In re* Marriage Cases, 183 P.3d 384, 452 (Cal. 2008). As of June 16, 2008, therefore, gay couples could marry in California. In November of that year, however, California passed a constitutional referendum to amend the California constitution to prohibit gay marriage (Proposition 8). Jesse McKinley & Laurie Goodstein, *Bans in 3 States on Gay Marriage*, N.Y. TIMES (Nov. 5, 2008),

marriage in California ended up in the federal courts, where, ultimately, the prohibition on gay marriage was overturned.[4] Of course, by 2015, in *Obergefell v. Hodges*, the United States Supreme Court declared that the right of gay people to marry was a fundamental right under the United States Constitution.[5] Then in 2022, in the now landmark case of *Dobbs v. Jackson Women's Health Organization* (overturning *Roe v. Wade*, which established the right to choose to have an abortion), Supreme Court Justice Clarence Thomas indicated that he was prepared to overturn the *Obergefell* case.[6] Remarkably, Congress acted quickly and passed the Respect for Marriage Act, which codifies the right of both same sex and interracial partners to marry.[7]

Through this cultural upheaval, we had gay friends and acquaintances who were getting married

---

https://www.nytimes.com/2008/11/06/us/politics/06marriage.html ?searchResultPosition=2. The California Supreme Court then upheld Proposition 8, which led to the oxymoronic result that gay people who married prior to Proposition 8 had valid marriages, but gay marriages were invalid after Proposition 8 was enacted. Strauss v. Horton, 207 P.3d 48, 122 (Cal. 2009).

[4] Perry v. Brown, 671 F.3d 1052, 1096 (9th Cir. 2012) (affirming the lower court's decision to overturn Proposition 8 as unconstitutional). The Supreme Court then heard the case but dismissed it on the basis that the plaintiffs bringing the case lacked standing. Hollingsworth v. Perry, 570 U.S. 693, 715 (2013).

[5] Obergefell v. Hodges, 576 U.S. 644, 681 (2015).

[6] Dobbs v. Jackson Women's Health Organization, 597 U.S. 215 (2022).

[7] President Joe Biden signed the *Respect for Marriage Act* into law on December 13, 2022. Respect for Marriage Act, P.L. 117–228, 136 Stat. 2305 (2022).

in various states. We had a gay friend and neighbor in Florida who had children with the help of a surrogate. Through him we met other gay couples having children through surrogacy and lesbian couples using sperm donors. Another friend had begun a child and family services agency and was counseling gay couples on family formation issues, including adoption and surrogacy arrangements. Suddenly, anything seemed possible. By about 2008, Mark and I began discussing the real possibility of starting a family together. But, of course, we were living in Florida where adoptions by gay people were still illegal.[8] Surrogacy seemed like the best route to having children. Then, we learned about the Florida surrogacy statute.[9]

As mentioned in the introduction, in Florida, for a surrogacy agreement to be honored and enforced by the courts, it has to be between a surrogate and intended parents who are married. Further the "commissioning woman" had to have fertility issues that would prevent her from carrying a healthy fetus.[10] Of course, when we were considering starting a family, gay people still could not be married in Florida.[11] Florida simply would not respect, honor, or

---

[8] FLA. STAT. ANN. § 63.042(3) (West 2014) (amended 2015).

[9] FLA. STAT. ANN. § 742.15 (West 2023).

[10] *Id.* The statute contains the additional requirement that the married couple essentially be infertile. *Id.* § 742.15(2)(a).

[11] In fact, in 2008, Florida held a referendum to amend its constitution to prohibit same-sex marriage. *See* McKinley & Goodstein, *supra* note 3. The amendment passed and same-sex marriage became patently unconstitutional. *See* McKinley & Goodstein, *supra* note 3. Civil unions were also prohibited. *See* FLA. CONST. art. I, § 27 (prohibiting recognition of same-sex

enforce surrogacy agreements where the intended parents were gay.

So, when we began our family formation planning, neither adoption nor surrogacy arrangements were legally condoned for gay people in Florida. Therefore, while Florida allowed gay men to be foster parents, there was no legally sanctioned way for gay men to become permanent legal parents in Florida.[12] However, the same was not true for gay women. While gay women still could not legally adopt, there was no legal prohibition on sperm donations that would allow gay women to become biological parents. But we as gay men were deadlocked. And so, we gambled.

As I mentioned, we knew other gay men in Florida who were forming their families with surrogates, despite the law clearly requiring intended parents to be married and infertile. Those parents gambled, they explained, that the surrogate would not try to break the surrogacy agreement in any way. Most importantly, they gambled with the chance that the surrogate would not try to gain custody of the child or children she would carry for the intended parent or parents. If that were to happen, the result might be a traditional custody battle with the intended parents fighting for custody against the surrogate.

---

marriages in the state). In 2014, a United States District Court found that provision of the Florida constitution unconstitutional under the United States Constitution. Brenner v. Scott, 999 F.Supp. 2d 1278, 1293 (N.D. Fla. 2014).

[12] FLA. STAT. ANN. § 63.042(3) (West 2014) (amended 2015); FLA. STAT. ANN. § 742.15 (West 2023).

This gamble meant that it was all the more important to be sure that intended parents found the right surrogate and trusted her completely. That, we figured, was crucial to the process anyway. And so, we joined the others in the gamble in 2011 and began our journey to parenthood through surrogacy.

In a surrogacy arrangement, a woman agrees to carry a baby (or multiples, as in our case) to term for an intended parent or parents. Crucial to the arrangement is that the surrogate agrees to have no parental rights and to transfer any parental rights she might ever have to the intended parent or parents. In traditional surrogacy arrangements, the egg is from the surrogate, making the surrogate the genetic mother of the child. The sperm is typically provided by the intended father, making him also a genetic parent.

In gestational surrogacy, the egg is donated by a third party. The sperm, again, is provided by the intended father. *In vitro fertilization* (IVF) is then used to transfer one or more embryos into the surrogate. So, in a gestational surrogacy arrangement, the surrogate is not a genetic parent. This fact minimizes risk for the intended parents because if a traditional custody battle were to ever ensue, it is likely that the genetic father would prevail over the surrogate. Because of that lowered risk, gestational surrogacy arrangements are now typically preferred.

Knowing our options, we looked more into the finer details of the process of transferring the embryos. In advising couples through the process, fertility doctors do not ordinarily recommend trying to have multiple babies. However, multiple embryos are often transferred after IVF because the rates of achieving a successful pregnancy can be low. If more than one embryo is transferred, the odds of having a successful pregnancy are increased. Because multiple embryos are often transferred, it is very possible that multiple babies are the result.

Learning all of this information, we set out to find the perfect egg donor and the perfect surrogate. That process is dizzying. There is a plethora of agencies ready to provide profiles of young women who are willing to be egg donors and others who are willing to be surrogates. The donors and surrogates are usually screened by the agencies, but there are generally no guaranties regarding the quality of the screening.

Furthermore, deciding on priorities for egg donors has its own dynamic. Does the egg donor need to be a college graduate? Does she need to be attractive? And what does attractive mean, really? Did we care about education, race, hair or eye color, musical or athletic abilities? We began working with an agency in Chicago. It took months for Mark and me to agree on a donor. The one we chose seemed amazing in every way. From her pictures and profile, she seemed spectacularly beautiful, smart, musical, creative, and athletic. We were beyond excited to start the personal journey with her.

Once my husband and I decided on our egg donor, we set out to find a surrogate. Through some local friends we found someone who seemed to be a perfect fit. She had three children of her own and had a successful career that demanded intelligence and empathy. She was smart and nurturing. She understood what pregnancy meant for her body and her life. Once again, we were thrilled.

After we completed the search for an egg donor and surrogate, we then turned to all of the required legal agreements. We had an agreement with a Chicago agency that sourced and vetted egg donors and surrogates, an agreement with the egg donor herself, and then an agreement with the surrogate. None of the agreements were simple, and we had to work through all the details with our attorney who specialized in these types of agreements.

We quickly learned various questions we had not considered. What would we all do if the baby was found to have special needs during the pregnancy? Could we abort? Would the surrogate agree to follow our wishes if we would? What if the surrogate was in an accident, and perhaps fell into a coma, but the baby was still viable? Would the surrogate's husband agree to let us keep her body alive to give birth to the child? These questions were profound and profoundly troubling for all parties involved. Even considering that last question almost made our surrogate back out. We finally hashed through it all, and we were ready to go.

In addition to the complexity from the legal documents, the medical process was not easy either.[13]

---

[13] *See generally What To Expect During the Surrogacy Medical Process*, AM. SURROGACY, https://www.americansurrogacy.com/surrogate/surrogacy-medical-process (last visited May 25, 2023)

There are psychological consultations for the intended parents and the surrogate, designed to ensure that everyone has thoroughly thought through, understands, and are prepared for the surrogacy journey. Then there are medical screenings and procedures—so many procedures. The egg donor has to be medically treated to hyper-ovulate and then have her eggs removed. With this hyper-ovulation, multiple eggs are generally retrieved, often between 10 and 15. The eggs are then fertilized in a lab setting, typically using the intended father's sperm, but perhaps donor sperm, to create embryos. The embryos are then evaluated for their quality by the fertility specialists, with the highest quality embryos chosen for the implantation. The surrogate will have been given medicine to thicken her uterine lining to prepare it for the embryo implantation.

If the process is to include a transfer of fresh embryos that were never frozen, then the surrogate has to have her body regulated and put on the same menstrual cycle as the egg donor. In that way, the egg retrieval from the egg donor can be immediately followed by fertilization, and then implantation of the embryo or embryos into the surrogate. Frozen embryos can be used, though, and in that case the surrogate does not need to be on the same cycle as the egg donor. For that reason, using frozen embryos can be more convenient, but many fertility experts think that a successful pregnancy is more likely if fresh

---

(providing a basic explanation of the medical procedures related to surrogacy).

embryos are used. Because multiple eggs are generally retrieved from an egg donor and then fertilized, some, if not all, of the embryos are generally frozen and stored for future use in any event. All in all, the preparations and procedures take months.

After those many months of preparation and planning, our first attempt failed. We simply did not have a successful pregnancy after our first embryo transfer. We were, however, prepared for this. We knew embryo transfers are not always successful and many intended parents go through multiple cycles. And so, we invested more time and underwent more procedures to undergo a second attempt.

After the various additional procedures, the second attempt failed as well. Undaunted, we carried on. On the eve of the third attempt, the doctors did their routine pre-implantation screening of our surrogate, including drug testing. They reported that this time our surrogate tested positive for amphetamines. The surrogate protested the results. She claimed that it must have been a mistake, but the clinic refused to proceed with the third attempt. We were shocked and devastated.

It took many months for us to even consider moving forward with the process all over again, but we did. The process was similarly challenging, but we found another egg donor and another surrogate. We prioritized the same factors for the egg donor—someone who seemed terrific in every way, beautiful, smart, musical, athletic. We chose a surrogate who was a primary school teacher. She seemed like a caring person, and one who had devoted herself to young children and families. We were more cautious this time, but still were optimistic. We went through all the legal hurdles of negotiating contracts for a second time. This time, working through the contracts was easier since we were familiar with the issues.

After all of that, though, once again the doctors found a problem with our new surrogate on the eve of the IVF procedure. Her uterine lining had not responded appropriately to the medicine and was not ready for an embryo transfer.

In looking into the cause, the surrogate confessed that she failed to take her medicine on a timely basis, as instructed. She was so sure she would get pregnant that she and her husband decided to take a cruise in the weeks before the insemination. With late nights out enjoying themselves, she had missed her morning medications repeatedly that week. And just like that, we had another strike-out. That surrogate promised us that she would be vigilant the next time around. She couldn't believe that missing a few—or several—doses would have made a difference. We were dumbfounded and livid all at the same time. Given how critical and demanding the process is, we refused to work with her again.

As time went by, we started to question why all of this was happening to us. Were we just not meant to be parents? Maybe it was all too much? Were we getting too old in our mid and late forties at that time? Could we go through the heartache and disappointment again?

We decided to keep going. We interviewed more potential surrogates with the help of our local attorney. With heightened skepticism, none of the candidates seemed right. It was during this third search for a surrogate that I remember feeling a sense of desperation. And then, we met the one.

Our neighbor, who had children through a surrogate, had been at a local playground with his son. He started chatting with a mom who was there with her son. When she asked our neighbor where his son's mom was, he told her he had worked with a surrogate and was a single dad. To his surprise, she then responded that she, in fact, had been a surrogate in the past. She had successfully delivered a healthy baby for a traditional couple in their forties who were struggling with fertility issues. Moreover, she was ready to do it again for the right couple. Hearing this, our friend immediately knew he needed to introduce us.

After getting to know each other, we all agreed to proceed. We found a new egg donor. After we completed all the legal hurdles, we underwent the appropriate procedures. Unfortunately, once again, repeated embryo transfers were unsuccessful. Our surrogate was amazing, though. Her strength and determination were infectious, and we simply kept trying.

Our clinic, however, was not so determined. We could not believe it. Adding to everything else that had gone wrong for us, our clinic essentially fired us. With so many failed attempts, they suggested we find another clinic, that maybe we would have more success elsewhere. And so, after everything we had been through, we did. Of course, we did.

Our new doctor had a high rate of successful IVF pregnancies. He also had an array of egg donors who had been vetted by his office. He suggested that for us, having been through several failed IVF and embryo transfer attempts, we should prioritize finding an egg donor who had donated eggs successfully—meaning her eggs resulted in a successful pregnancy for a surrogate. That narrowed our search for a donor, but we still were able to find one who met that criteria that we thought would be terrific.

In meeting with us, our new fertility doctor also insisted we transfer only one embryo. Knowing the difficulty, we had in the past, I challenged him on this. We had been through so much and had so many failed attempts. I encouraged him to reconsider to give ourselves better odds of success at getting our surrogate pregnant. He compromised and agreed that if the first embryo transfer of one embryo failed, then he would transfer two in the next attempt.

Sure enough, we had yet another failure. Keeping to his word, our doctor transferred two embryos the next time. And that is when the magic happened.

After years of trying, multiple egg donors, multiple surrogates, endless medical screenings and procedures, and well over one hundred thousand dollars spent, our surrogate was finally successfully pregnant. Our incredible twin boys were born in June of 2014. Looking back at the experience, as difficult as it was, every minute and every challenge was worth it in every way.

# CHAPTER 2
# INTENDED PARENTS

**Tales from the Field: Pregnancy Difficulties Lead to Surrogacy**

Many traditional couples struggle with fertility and pregnancy and turn to surrogacy as a way to form their families. One husband and wife pursuing surrogacy as I write this had difficulties with the pregnancy of their first child. The mother developed preeclampsia early in the pregnancy.

A little more than halfway through a full term, the doctors advised that they would need to deliver the baby at that time, or the lives of both the mother and baby could be lost. The couple went forward with the pre-mature delivery, and the lives of both the courageous mother and the beautiful baby girl were saved.

The husband and wife had always wanted more than one child. So, a few years after the birth of their daughter and after much discussion and soul-searching, they decided to pursue a surrogacy arrangement. The planning went well. All the details were agreed upon and the surrogate became pregnant after the first embryo transfer.

Though it was not part of the plan, ironically, the wife also then became pregnant at about the same time. As a result, the couple had two healthy children born within weeks of one another, one carried by the surrogate, the other carried by the wife.

Surrogacy is driven by the intended parent or parents who are seeking to form a family. If that is you, then traditional family formation is either not possible (like it wasn't for us as gay men), or carries high medical risks (as it does for that traditional couple where carrying a baby presents high risks for both the mother and the child).

For most intended parents looking to surrogacy as a possibility, the details of a surrogacy arrangement will be unfamiliar, and there is a fairly high learning curve. This chapter is meant to help intended parents understand the process better, and navigate the challenges with grace and patience. It is crucial to note from the outset that a surrogacy arrangement is really a collaboration among an array of different people all helping the intended parents achieve their goal of parenthood. Collaboration, cooperation, and trust among these parties are crucial to success.

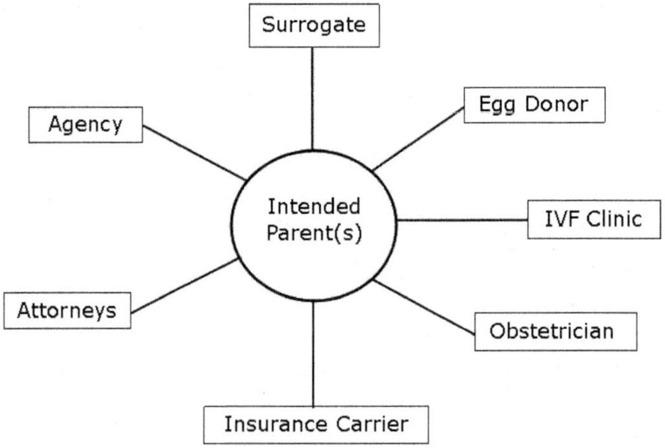

## 1. OTHER ROADS TO FAMILY FORMATION

Like us, intended parents contemplating surrogacy likely will also have seriously considered other roads to family formation. Foster care and adoption are two other avenues to parenthood. As *The New York Times* described foster parenting, "[t]he need is real."[1] Hundreds of thousands of children are in foster care in the United States. Foster parents report that the experience of providing a loving home to a child in need is incredibly rewarding, despite the hurdles involved in getting licensed.[2] In 2020, the U.S. Department of Health and Human Services reported that there were over 400,000 children in foster care in the United States.[3]

Many children are adopted out of the foster care system, but many are also adopted through private agencies or through overseas adoptions. In 2020, the U.S. Department of Health and Human Services authored a report on statistics related to foster care and adoption. That report showed that the number of adoptions out of foster care in the United States was 66,000 in 2019, up from 53,400 in 2010.[4]

---

1 Benjamin J. Dueholm, *How (and Why) to Become a Foster Parent*, N.Y. TIMES (Apr. 18, 2020), https://www.nytimes.com/article/foster-care.html.

2 *Id.*

3 U.S. DEPARTMENT OF HEALTH AND HUMAN SERVICES, CHILDREN'S BUREAU, THE AFCARS REPORT 1 (No. 28, 2021), https://www.acf.hhs.gov/sites/default/files/documents/cb/afcars report28.pdf.

4 U.S. DEPARTMENT OF HEALTH AND HUMAN SERVICES, CHILDREN'S BUREAU, TRENDS IN FOSTER CARE AND ADOPTION: FY

Like all roads to family formation, foster care and adoption come with their own pros and cons. Each intended parent will need to work through those issues for themselves.[5] At the top of the list of benefits with both fostering and adoption is the reward of providing a child in need with a nurturing and supportive home.

Costs of adoption can be a pro or a con as costs vary widely. Adopting a child out of a state foster care system may be very low cost and may include some added benefits for the adopting family like monthly financial support and free in-state college tuition for the child.[6] But private or international adoptions can easily cost tens of thousands of dollars, reaching $50,000 or more.[7]

Again, with some factors, intended parents need to consider for themselves if concerns are a pro or a con. With foster care and adoption, infants are often unavailable. And so many foster relationships and

---

2010–FY 2019 1 (2020), https://www.acf.hhs.gov/cb/report/trends-foster-care-adoption-fy-2010-2019.

5 *See generally* U.S. DEPARTMENT OF HEALTH AND HUMAN SERVICES, CHILDREN'S BUREAU, FAMILIES CONSIDERING FOSTER CARE AND ADOPTION (2019), https://www.childwelfare.gov/resources/families-considering-foster-care-and-adoption/ (discussing questions that potential foster parents should consider).

6 Florida, for example, provides both of those benefits and more. Fla. Dep't of Child. & Fams., *Benefits of Adopting Florida's Children*, MYFLFAMILIES, https://adoptflorida.org/considering-adoption/benefits-of-state-adoption/ (last visited June 1, 2023).

7 *See generally DePaul Community Resources, The Cost of Private Adoption vs the Cost of Adoption from Foster Care* (2025), https://www.depaulcr.org/cost-private-adoption-vs-adoption-foster-care/ (last visited April 11, 2025).

adoptions involve toddlers or older children. Those children can come to their new family with potential emotional issues that will need to be addressed. For example, children in the foster care system likely will have experienced some amount of emotional trauma resulting from their birth family being unavailable to care for them.[8] Foster parents are counseled that they need to be supportive of the birth family of the foster child and to be prepared for a reunification of the foster child with their birth family. When adopting a toddler or an older child, intended parents should consider the dynamics of parenting children who have experienced such separation and loss.

And if the intended parents already have children, considering the way foster or adopted children will fit in with the existing family is important. One set of intended parents seriously considered fostering a middle school girl who had been the victim of sexual abuse, but who herself had already become sexually active. They decided that they simply didn't want to take what they perceived to be the risks associated with bringing that child into their home where they already had a daughter and a son who were of a similar age.

If fostering or adoption do not seem like the right fit for you or your family, then surrogacy may well be the answer. Many intended parents opt for surrogacy because they want a genetic connection with their

---

[8] U.S. DEPARTMENT OF HEALTH AND HUMAN SERVICES, CHILDREN'S BUREAU, HELPING YOUR CHILD TRANSITION FROM FOSTER CARE TO ADOPTION (2018), https://www.childwelfare.gov/resources/helping-your-child-transition-foster-care-adoption/.

child. If you have gotten to the point where surrogacy seems like the right fit for you, then you need to understand the process.

## 2. THE SURROGACY PROCESS

At its most basic, in a surrogacy arrangement, a woman agrees to carry a baby (or multiples in our case) to term for the intended parent or parents. Crucial to the arrangement is that the surrogate agrees to have no parental rights and to transfer any parental rights she might ever have to the intended parent or parents.

In *traditional surrogacy* arrangements, the egg used comes from the surrogate, making the surrogate the genetic mother of the child. The sperm is typically provided by the intended father, making him also a genetic parent.

In *gestational surrogacy*, the egg is either the intended mother's or it is donated by a third party. The sperm, again, is typically provided by the intended father, but in rare cases might also be donated by a third party if the intended father has medical issues that prevent him from using his sperm.

In some ways, traditional surrogacy is easier than gestational surrogacy because there is no need to find an additional egg donor. The traditional surrogate also provides the egg. But that also makes the traditional surrogate the genetic mother of the child. In the nightmare scenario that the surrogate decides to break her agreement with the intended parent or parents, and fight for parental rights, including custody of the child, a genetic mother will have a stronger case than a gestational surrogate, with no genetic relationship to the child. In most gestational surrogacy cases, even if the intended mother is not the genetic parent, the intended father, as the sperm provider, is the genetic father. His rights to custody would typically prevail over those of the surrogate, who is not a genetic parent. Because of that lowered risk of a surrogate prevailing in a custody battle, gestational surrogacy arrangements are now generally preferred over traditional surrogacy.

A traditional surrogate fought for parental rights and custody of the child born in the famous *Baby M* case, one of the earliest surrogacy cases from the late 1980s.[9] Because the traditional surrogate was the genetic mother of the child, she had a better chance of prevailing in the battle over parental rights. In the end, the traditional surrogate lost the case, and custody did end up with the intended parents, but not until a lengthy court battle was waged. The *Baby M* case involves a dizzying array of facts that are horrifying to imagine for any intended parent, including the fact that the surrogate ran off with the baby and went into hiding. The case is discussed in more detail below as a case study in what can go wrong with a traditional surrogacy, or really with any surrogacy. It is a cautionary tale for why intended parents have to proceed with extreme care

---

[9] *In re* Baby M, 537 A.2d 1227, 1238–39 (N.J. 1988).

both in finding the right surrogate and in structuring the relationship appropriately.

So, let's assume you proceed with a gestational surrogacy arrangement. You will go through the process of selecting an egg donor, if necessary, a surrogate, and a fertility clinic. None of that is likely to happen quickly and may not happen easily either. Again, it took my husband and I months of sorting through egg donor profiles to agree on the right egg donor for us. We had similar lengthy soul-searching exercises when it came to selecting our surrogates (hopefully, you won't need more than one like we did).

So, at this point, as throughout the process, you need to have patience and keep focus on what is really important to you. We began our search by thinking of the physical and mental qualities of the egg donor that our child might inherit. That is, of course, important, but by the end of our process we had prioritized finding an egg donor with a proven history of donating eggs that resulted in a live birth.

You might decide to work with a surrogacy agency to help you find your egg donor and surrogate. Alternatively, you might find a fertility clinic that can assist you with those choices. You will also need to find your own attorney to help you navigate the contracts involved with the surrogate and the egg donor. Your attorney might be able to put you in touch with potential egg donors and surrogates. A quick Google search will yield a wide array of agencies and other professionals across the country dedicated to helping intended parents form their families.

In our case, we began with an agency based in Chicago, ConceiveAbilities.[10] They had excellent professionals who helped us think through the process, and provided us a database of vetted egg donors and surrogates available to us.

Keep in mind, through all of this, that you will be paying the bills for any agency, attorney, or other professionals you enlist to help you with the process. The fees, of course, are in addition to the compensation for the surrogate and any egg or sperm donor. Agency and professional fees can be well worth it, but proceed cautiously and interview a variety of professionals before deciding which you will choose.

When interviewing those professionals, be candid about your needs and your budget. Ask questions about their fee structures, and see if they will give you references. Then follow up with those references to see if the professionals were helpful to other intended parents.

ConceiveAbilities, for example, in mid-2023, stated on their website that new surrogates can expect to be compensated with as much as $72,000.[11] That amount would be paid by the intended parents. To make costs simpler, however, ConceiveAbilities also has an "all in" fee that includes compensation and certain medical fees for the surrogate (not including

---

[10] *See* CONCEIVEABILITIES, https://www.conceiveabilities.com/parents/parents-and-surrogate/cost-and-fees/ (last visited June 1, 2023) for more information.

[11] *How Much Do Surrogate Mothers Get Paid*, CONCEIVEABILITIES, https://www.conceiveabilities.com/surrogates/surrogate-mother-pay/ (last visited June 1, 2023).

IVF), and compensation for the agency for coordinating the arrangements. In early 2025, that fee was set at $197,500.[12] Intended parents will want to focus on the details of any cost arrangements of that sort and be sure to understand exactly what is included and what is not. But, in short, surrogacy entails significant costs.

Once you have selected the egg donor (if necessary), your surrogate and your fertility clinic, you will all likely be asked to undergo a mental health consultation. Such a consultation may well be required by the state statute that will govern your arrangement. That consultation is designed to make sure that each of the parties understands all of the dynamics involved in the egg donation, the surrogacy process, the resulting childbirth and parenthood. Moreover, all the parties need to understand the risks, medical and psychological, of the process.

For egg donors, they need to understand that they likely will have no contact with any child born with their egg, or may have contact under very limited conditions. Contact may be agreed upon by the parties, for example, after the child reaches a certain age, or if there are medical emergencies that might require a compatible blood or organ donor.

For the surrogate, it is crucial that she understand that she will be carrying the child for the intended parents. She will be expected to waive any and all

---

[12] *Gestational Surrogacy Cost & Fees*, CONCEIVEABILITIES, https://www.conceiveabilities.com/parents/parents-and-surrogate/cost-and-fees/ (last visited April 11, 2025).

parental rights once the child is born, including any rights to custody of any sort. The surrogate will need to understand that any bond that is created through carrying the child through to birth may make it very difficult to give the child over to the intended parents when he or she is born.

For the intended parent or parents, the obligation to assume the parental rights of the child born are key. That may seem obvious, but there have been cases, especially when a child is born with medical complications or health concerns, when an intended parent no longer wants custody of the child. In other cases, the intended parents break up or divorce mid-pregnancy and, again, one or both then no longer want to take parental rights over the child born. The obligation of parenthood for the intended parents is crucial. Surrogates typically are not prepared to become the parent of the child born through surrogacy, with a lifetime of obligations. If the intended parents break their agreement to assume parental rights, the surrogate may be faced with the option of taking on parental rights.

Assuming all goes well, the process will continue, and all the parties will work with attorneys to discuss, negotiate, and agree upon their respective contracts. The attorneys for all the parties are paid by the intended parents. The contracts involved will cover the basics, like how much and how the egg donor and the surrogate will be paid. The contracts will also delve into many deeper and complex issues.

For the egg donor, the contract will detail the extent of the anonymity of the donor. The contract will likely outline conditions upon which the parties agree when the egg donor might be contacted by any child born from her egg.

For the surrogate, a wide array of issues will be addressed, including what happens if she gets pregnant with more than one embryo, or what happens if there is some reason why either the surrogate or the intended parents want to terminate a pregnancy. A contract with a surrogate will likely even detail lifestyle choices for the surrogate to ensure a healthy birth—commitments like not smoking or drinking alcohol. Details of the egg donor and surrogacy agreements are discussed in later chapters.

Again, assuming all goes well, and that the parties come to agreement on their contracts, the medical work will begin. The egg donor, the surrogate, and the intended father (or sperm donor) will go through medical pre-screenings. The egg donor then will begin medication to hyper-stimulate her ovaries to produce multiple eggs. The surrogate will be given medication to prepare her uterine lining to receive an embryo transfer.

If the egg donor's medications have worked, the eggs will be retrieved from the egg donor. The intended father will likely provide the necessary sperm. At that stage, in vitro fertilization (IVF) is used to fertilize the eggs to create viable embryos.

Within three to five days of embryonic growth, the embryos are then typically assigned grades that correspond to their quality. Higher quality "A" or "B" graded embryos have a better chance of resulting in a successful pregnancy than, for example, a "C" graded embryo. Quality is determined somewhat subjectively by embryologists and fertility physicians by assessing whether the embryonic cells are dividing as they should, and whether the resulting cells show any fragmentation. Fragmentation refers to any contents of the embryonic cells not being re-captured into new cells as the cells divide. In other words, fragments of the original cells are left out from the new cells. When the time comes, be sure to talk to your fertility experts about the grading of your embryos to make sure you don't waste time and effort—and money—transferring lower quality embryos that have a very small likelihood of resulting in a successful pregnancy.

Embryologists and fertility doctors can also use pre-implantation genetic testing on the embryos to assess whether an embryo might have a propensity for a particular genetic disease, for example cystic fibrosis. Some intended parents, especially those with a genetic disease in their family history, may want to undertake those genetic tests and then not use embryos that are likely to result in a child with that genetic disease.

Experts can likewise use pre-implantation testing to determine the sex of the embryos. In that case, the experts look for whether the embryos exhibit two X chromosomes, indicating a female, or one X and one Y, indicating a male. Again, some intended parents may want to know this information and then choose to transfer the embryos that are the sex that they would prefer for their child.

In our particular case, we told our fertility doctor not to tell us the sex of the embryos, but simply to use the highest quality embryos so that we had the best chance of a successful pregnancy, regardless of sex. Just like so many of the decisions related to family formation through surrogacy, like choosing the qualities you want in an egg donor, these kinds of decisions are very personal. You may choose to keep these decisions private among only your most trusted friends and family.

When any pre-implantation embryonic testing has been completed and you have chosen which embryo or embryos to transfer, your fertility doctor will then complete the transfer of one or more embryos into the uterine lining of the surrogate. You, your surrogate, and your fertility doctor can discuss whether it makes sense for you to be there when the transfer is done. In some ways, this is the magic moment when your child's future begins.

We always wanted to be present for that moment, and our surrogates and doctors always agreed to allow for that. In almost every case of our embryo transfers, we were physically in the room when the procedure happened. As I mentioned in our own surrogacy story, we had several failed embryo transfers. During our last embryo transfer, the successful one when our children were transferred into our surrogate, however, we were living in London where I was teaching law for a semester abroad. Our fertility doctor was amazing, though, and immediately suggested that we, essentially, have a Zoom embryo transfer. In that way we were electronically present via video conference for what we have always now referred to as the trans-Atlantic insemination.

| The Surrogacy Process at a Glance |
|---|
| 1. Decide whether **surrogacy is the right option**; |
| 2. Consider using **a surrogacy agency** to facilitate the process, including sourcing an egg donor and a surrogate |
| 3. Find and **agree upon an egg donor**, if one is needed; |
| 4. Find and **agree with a surrogate** to work together; |
| 5. Find and **agree upon a fertility doctor** and clinic; |
| 6. **Arrange for mental health consultations** for intended parents, surrogate, and egg donor so that all understand and are prepared for the process, risks, and dynamics; |
| 7. Hire and work with attorneys to **negotiate contract with any donor** (typically a different attorney for each party); |
| 8. Hire and work with attorneys to **negotiate contract with your surrogate** (typically a different one for each party); |
| 9. Assess **whether to procure insurance** to cover the pregnancy and birth; |

10. **Begin medical health pre-screenings** for egg donor, surrogate, and intended father (assuming he is providing the sperm);
11. **Begin medications for egg donor** in anticipation of egg retrieval;
12. **Begin medications for surrogate** in anticipation of embryo implantation;
13. **Sperm donation** is taken;
14. **Egg donation** is taken;
15. **IVF** occurs to create viable embryos;
16. Pre-implantation **genetic testing for genetic diseases** can be conducted;
17. Pre-implantation testing can be conducted to **assess the sex** of each embryo, if desired;
18. **Embryos are graded**;
19. High quality **embryos are transferred** to surrogate with hopes of a successful pregnancy!

## 3. THE CLASSIC SURROGACY CASE STUDY: *BABY M*

The famous case of *Baby M* made the world take notice of surrogacy. The case is instructive even today as it illustrates both the nature of the arrangement between the intended parents and the surrogate, and also some of the inherent risks involved with surrogacy. Surrogacy was quite novel forty years ago. Indeed, the court considering the case referred to surrogacy as "a new way of bringing children into a family."[13] Despite the novelty of the arrangement, the intended parents and the surrogate were connected through a surrogacy agency.[14]

In the *Baby M* case, a married couple that were struggling to have their own biological children sought the help of a surrogate.[15] The couple, William and Elizabeth Stern, met while they were each earning their Ph.D. degree at the University of Michigan.[16] Later, Elizabeth went on to pursue a medical degree and a medical residency.[17] The Sterns put off having children.[18] When the couple decided to pursue a family, Elizabeth learned that she might have multiple sclerosis.[19] As a result, Elizabeth did not dare to have children naturally due to the associated medical risks.[20] While both William and Elizabeth wanted to have children, William had an additional motivation to become a father.[21] William's family had been destroyed in the Holocaust, and he fervently wanted to continue his family line.[22]

Mary Beth Whitehead agreed to be the surrogate mother for the Sterns.[23] Mary Beth was married at

---

[13] *In re Baby M*, 537 A.2d at 1234.

[14] *Id.* at 1235.

[15] *Id.* at 1235–36.

[16] *Id.* at 1235.

[17] *Id.*

[18] *Id.*

[19] *Id.*

[20] *Id.*

[21] *Id.*

[22] *Id.*

[23] *Id.*

the time and already had her own children.[24] She decided to be a surrogate even before meeting the Sterns and had unsuccessfully worked with another couple previously.[25] The court deciding the case explained that Mary Beth had become a surrogate because of her sympathy for couples who could not have a child, her desire to give the "gift of life," and her interest in supplementing her own family's income with the amount that she would earn as compensation.[26] Mary Beth charged $10,000.[27] The agency's fee was $7,500.[28]

At the time of the surrogacy arrangement, all the parties were living in New Jersey where there was no statute addressing surrogacy at all. Nonetheless, the parties signed a contract outlining all of their rights and responsibilities related to the surrogacy, assuming those commitments would be binding. Those commitments included the amount of compensation the Sterns would pay Mary Beth, and the crucial requirement that Mary Beth give up any and all parental rights and transfer custody of the child to the Sterns immediately after the child's birth.[29]

After the baby was born, the Sterns named the child Melissa.[30] Unfortunately for the Sterns, Mary

---

[24] *Id.* at 1237.

[25] *Id.* at 1236.

[26] *Id.*

[27] *Id.* at 1235.

[28] *Id.*

[29] *Id.*

[30] *Id.* at 1236.

Beth decided to keep Melissa after she was born.[31] The Sterns brought suit against Mary Beth to enforce the surrogacy contract and to obtain custody of Melissa. The court entered an order for a hearing. But while the process server was serving the Whiteheads with the court order, the Whiteheads smuggled the child out a back window and ran off with her to Florida.[32]

The Whiteheads remained in Florida for several months, living with relatives and in motels.[33] During that time, Mary Beth periodically contacted William to try to get him to agree to let Mary Beth have custody of the child.[34] Throughout those conversations Mary Beth expressed desperation, threatening to kill herself and the child.[35] Finally, with the help of the authorities, the child was apprehended in Florida and the Sterns regained custody in New Jersey.[36]

New Jersey had jurisdiction of the matter because all of the parties lived in New Jersey at the time of the surrogacy arrangement and because Melissa was born there. The superior court ruled in favor of the Sterns and enforced the surrogacy agreement. Mary Beth appealed, and the Supreme Court of New Jersey refused to enforce the surrogacy agreement. The Supreme Court of New Jersey ruled that surrogacy

---

[31] *Id.*

[32] *Id.* at 1237.

[33] *Id.*

[34] *Id.*

[35] *Id.*

[36] *Id.*

contracts were void in New Jersey because public policy forbids them.[37] In addition, the court opined that such arrangements may be "degrading to women,"[38] hinting that surrogacy commodifies women by turning them into vessels that can be bought and sold.[39]

The court discussed the adoption statutes in New Jersey and found that those statutes allowed the woman who gave birth to a child an opportunity after birth to change her mind about whether or not to give the child up for adoption.[40] The court reasoned that since the adoption laws provided this choice after the birth of the child, a surrogacy agreement should not be allowed to take away the birth mother's right to decide after birth to keep the child.[41] To rule otherwise, the court wrote, would be to condone a

---

[37] *Id.* at 1246–50.

[38] *Id.* at 1234.

[39] Opponents of surrogacy argue that the choice to become a surrogate isn't a choice at all. Opponents point out that many women of lower economic standing may feel coerced into becoming a surrogate for economic reasons and argue that by becoming a surrogate mother, the woman reduces herself to a marketable product. This debate takes on more focus in India where many women live in stark poverty and being a surrogate can mean earning two thousand times more than the next best paying alternative. Advocates for surrogacy argue that being a surrogate is a wonderful and economically empowering option for these women. Kevin Voigt, Mallika Kapur, & Lonzo Cook, *Wombs for Rent: India's Surrogate Mother Boomtown*, CNN (Nov. 3, 2013, 8:00 PM) http://www.cnn.com/2013/11/03/world/asia/india-surrogate-mother-industry/.

[40] *In re Baby M*, 537 A.2d at 1242.

[41] *Id.* at 1240.

market for the sale of babies.[42] The court stated: "The evils inherent in baby-bartering are loathsome for a myriad of reasons. . . . Baby-selling potentially results in the exploitation of all the parties involved."[43]

This result for the Sterns started a custody battle with the Whiteheads. In this case, Mary Beth was a traditional surrogate, meaning that the Sterns had used William's sperm to fertilize Mary Beth's egg. This meant that Mary Beth was not only a gestational carrier, but also the genetic mother of the child. Thus, with the surrogacy contract voided by the court, both the genetic father (William) and the genetic mother (Mary Beth) had a claim for the custody of the child.[44] In the end, the Sterns won custody of the child.

In the United States, as the *Baby M* case demonstrates, surrogacy is controversial. Some states have historically treated surrogacy like the state of New Jersey, as something akin to baby selling and the commodification of women and therefore something that should not be condoned or supported.

Michigan is an example of one state that still has criminal penalties for the parties to a surrogacy arrangement. But more and more states have now provided that surrogacy should be allowed, but should also be regulated. In fact, even New Jersey

---

42 *Id.* at 1242.

43 *Id.* at 1241–42.

44 *Id.* at 1251.

now permits and regulates surrogacy under a surrogacy statute.

Knowing the laws of your state is therefore crucial. If your state is not supportive of surrogacy, you should consider choosing to have your arrangements governed by the laws of a state that is supportive. For such a choice to be upheld, the parties typically need some connections with the chosen state that makes that choice reasonable and not just a way to avoid the laws of your own state. A survey of the surrogacy laws of each state is present later in this book in Chapter 6.

As the *Baby M* case also illustrates, state law is one major risk that must be managed in the surrogacy arrangement. A second risk present in the *Baby M* case was the fact that the surrogate was actually the genetic mother of *Baby M.* This connection likely strengthened her emotional tie to the baby, making it harder for her to part with the baby after birth. Moreover, it also gave the court a strong factor to consider in granting ultimate custody to the surrogate instead of the intended parents. If the parties had used an egg donor, instead of the eggs of the surrogate, then that may have prevented some of the bonding between the surrogate and the baby. It also would have eliminated the genetic connection that a court may use to grant custody or other parental rights to the surrogate.[45]

---

[45] In *Johnson v. Calvert*, 851 P.2d 776, 783 (Cal. 1993) the Supreme Court of California enforced a gestational surrogacy agreement largely based on the intent of the parties to the surrogacy agreement. The court found support for its conclusion in

A final cautionary aspect of the *Baby M* case is that, despite all reasonable steps taken to plan for a successful surrogacy arrangement, sometimes things go wrong. In the *Baby M* case, things went terribly wrong. The surrogate reneged on her contractual commitment to abandon any and all parental rights and willingly transfer custody of the child born over to the intended parents. The Whiteheads essentially kidnapped Melissa and ran off to another state with her. The intended parents did what they had to do to assert their rights and their interests. They worked with their attorney and went to court.

Carefully working through all the surrogacy arrangements in advance, including the mental health consultations and the contractual discussions, can help prevent this kind of negative outcome. But intended parents have to recognize that there are no guaranties and there are always risks. Of course, that is true with any journey to family formation. There are always risks.

---

*Calvert* in Majorie Maguire Shultz, *Reproductive Technology and Intent-based Parenthood: An Opportunity for Gender Neutrality*, 1990 WIS. L. REV. 297, 323 (1990). The court quoted Professor Shultz: "Within the context of artificial reproductive techniques, intentions that are voluntarily chosen, deliberate, express and bargained-for ought presumptively to determine legal parenthood."

# CHAPTER 3
# THE SURROGATE

Surrogacy would simply not be possible without the surrogate. We are so grateful every day that our surrogate was willing to work with us and give us the gift of carrying our children. This chapter will focus on the surrogate and hopefully will be helpful for any woman considering becoming a surrogate and any professional who might provide counsel to surrogates. Intended parents will want to peruse this chapter too to understand better some of the issues that face a surrogate.

## 1. SURROGATE STORIES

As a doula, a woman's healthcare professional focused on issues related to pregnancy and childbirth, our surrogate had told us from the outset that she had always wanted to help other people in need create their families. Moreover, she and her same-sex partner conceived their son with the help of a third-party sperm donor. Because of that, she felt like being a surrogate was a way to pay forward the help she had received, help she could give to others in need.

She had worked with a traditional opposite-sex married couple who, like the Sterns in the Baby M case, were professionals who had put off having children until they were in their 40s, and then discovered that they needed help to carry a baby. Just a few years after that experience, our surrogate was ready to give that gift again to the right family.

That's when we were introduced. We were so lucky to have met her. She was beyond helpful in every way and really represents, in our view, the best version of what a surrogate can be.

Because our surrogate had been through the process, and was a doula, she was an expert in the issues related to surrogacy. She'd already negotiated through a surrogacy contract and gone through all the psychological and medical consultations and procedures.

We would be at the fertility doctor's office discussing our procedures and she could have led the conversations and explained (maybe sometimes better than the doctor because she would simplify things) what we could or should expect. She was eternally optimistic and her enthusiasm for all things about family formation gave us strength and courage to move forward even as things didn't always turn out as we hoped.

As mentioned earlier, by the time we met her, we had worked with two other surrogates who didn't work out, and several failed embryo transfers. Moreover, even with her, we had a few failed transfers. Nonetheless, our surrogate was awesome. She was always ready to try again, was undeterred, and infectiously energetic. I remember so many conversations with her on our way to appointments when she would describe the joys of parenting and give advice on how to manage young children. Her off handed discussions made the process seem successful even when it hadn't been yet. She was certain that she would become pregnant, and her positive attitude was crucial to our ultimate success.

Of course, not every surrogate is a women's health professional and for most surrogates the first time will involve just as steep a learning curve as there is for the first-time intended parent. Nonetheless, stories from others who have been a surrogate can be inspiring and can underscore why being a surrogate might be the right choice for someone considering it.

**Tales from the Field: A Super-Surrogate**

Another surrogate with whom I spoke was a surrogate four different times. She came to surrogacy with a different story than our surrogate. She explained to me that she had suffered a miscarriage of her own child early on in her life.

After she and her husband then had three children of their own successfully, she just knew she wanted to help others who had difficulties having children. She commented that to begin with her husband was skeptical, but when they got to know their first intended family, he became very supportive.

That surrogate added that the compensation involved allowed her some financial freedom so that she could quit her regular job, and be at home with her own children, another benefit for both her and her husband. Her first experience went so smoothly and was so gratifying, that she decided to do it again and become a super-surrogate.

By the time I spoke with her, this woman had given birth to seven children, three of her own and four acting as a surrogate for other families. She described her surrogacy experiences as simply "so fulfilling." Further, she "adores" the families she helped, and was "a little sad" when she decided it was likely finally time for her to stop being a surrogate. But, like our surrogate, she is in contact with the families with which she worked, and finds those connections to be powerful and uplifting.

As these stories suggest, being a surrogate can be an empowering way to help others form their families. At the same time, it can also be a way for a surrogate to earn compensation to help achieve personal goals.

Nonetheless, surrogacy has been and continues to be controversial. Anyone considering surrogacy should consider these issues before proceeding.

## 2. CRITICISMS OF SURROGACY

A discussion of surrogacy would be incomplete without considering the criticisms surrogacy has received over the years. At its core, arguments against surrogacy have centered on protecting the women who might agree to be surrogates from being exploited. Power dynamics, class, sex, and race are all at stake in this discussion.

Commercial surrogacy emerged in the United States around 1980.[1] Again, one of the earliest reported cases in the United States is the *Baby M* case from 1988.[2] Recall that in the *Baby M* case, discussed in Chapter 2, the New Jersey Supreme Court refused to enforce the surrogacy agreement based on fears that the arrangement amounted to selling babies, resulting in the "exploitation of all parties involved."[3]

As surrogacy was emerging as a viable avenue for family formation in those early years, many feminists and other women's advocates argued that surrogacy arrangements could never include true consent of the surrogate to relinquish parental rights of any child born.[4] It would be difficult, they argued, for a surrogate to understand in advance what it would mean to give up custody of a child she would birth.[5]

Moreover, any surrogacy arrangements could exploit and commodify vulnerable women.[6] Women who struggle financially would agree to become

---

[1] *See generally* Courtney G. Joslin, *Surrogacy and the Politics of Pregnancy*, 14 HARV. L. & POL'Y REV. 365 (2020), for a discussion of the history of surrogacy and evolving opinions about the arrangement.

[2] *In re* Baby M, 537 A.2d 1227 (N.J. 1988).

[3] *Id.* at 1242.

[4] Karen Busby & Delaney Vun, *Revisiting* The Handmaid's Tale*: Feminist Theory Meets Empirical Research on Surrogate Mothers*, 26 CAN. J. FAM. L. 13, 17 (2010), https://femlaw.queensu.ca/sites/flswww/files/uploaded_files/Law692Law693/law693Winter2018/Busby_2010.pdf.

[5] *Id.*

[6] *See* Douglas NeJaime, *The Nature of Parenthood*, 126 YALE L.J. 2260, 2301 (2017).

surrogates, effectively renting out their bodies in the process, all for the benefit of a more affluent group of intended parents who could afford to pay for those services. Allowing surrogacy could allow wealthy people to take advantage of women of lesser means.

With this power imbalance, critics argued, intended parents often get surrogates to allow the intended parents to control certain aspects of the surrogate's behavior.[7] Benignly, that might mean insuring that the surrogate's behavior during pregnancy is in the best interest of the developing fetus. So, behavioral restrictions like a surrogate agreeing not to smoke or drink alcohol while pregnant are common. But even more control can be exerted by intended parents or even the courts. Issues like the intended parents making medical decisions for the surrogate if the health of the fetus is involved are often discussed in surrogacy arrangements. If courts enforce these contractual provisions, it can mean that a surrogate would no longer have control over decisions affecting her own body.[8]

**Criticisms of Surrogacy**

As surrogacy was emerging as a viable avenue for family formation, many women's advocates largely had these primary concerns.

---

[7] Sara L. Ainsworth, *Bearing Children, Bearing Risks: Feminist Leadership for Progressive Regulation of Compensated Surrogacy in the United States*, 89 WASH. L. REV. 1077, 1089–90 (2014).

[8] *Id.*

1. **Consent**—whether the surrogate could truly consent in advance to give up custody of the child she would birth;
2. **Exploitation**—surrogates might be exploited and agree to the arrangement, including the physical dangers inherent in pregnancy, out of economic necessity; and
3. **Commodification**—surrogates being *commodified* by agreeing to trade their reproductive capabilities for pay, and then could be subjected to bodily control by intended parents or even courts.

Some advocates for women's rights point out that it's the surrogate who bears the most risk in a surrogacy arrangement. "[I]t is the women who hold the least power and face the highest risk of economic exploitation who bear the most significant risks in these arrangements."[9] For example, pregnancy can result in health complications for the surrogate who might ultimately suffer lasting medical affects from a difficult pregnancy.

The power imbalance between relatively wealthy intended parents and their surrogates becomes even more acute in developing countries, discussed later in Chapter 12, where the economic incentive for women to become surrogates is even more dramatic. In India, for example, women can earn several times an

---

[9] *Id.* at 1077.

average annual salary for serving as a surrogate.[10] Because of this and other factors like a well-developed healthcare system, commercial surrogacy in India surged in popularity about a decade ago. International surrogacy has now been officially banned in India out of concerns that the surrogates were being exploited.[11]

Race has also played a complicated role in the way some people think about surrogacy. The history of the United States includes the reality that black women who were slaves often had no legal parental or custody rights relating to their own children.[12] Instead, their children became the property of the enslaved mother's owners.[13] This kind of historic disenfranchisement of women from the motherhood of the children they birth is compared to a surrogate agreeing to give up children that they birth for economic reasons. Some scholars see both practices as similarly denigrating and exploitative.[14]

---

10 See *Nayanthara-Vignesh Controversy: What Laws Regulate Surrogacy in India*, INDIAN EXPRESS (Oct. 13, 2022, 3:43 PM), https://indianexpress.com/article/explained/what-laws-regulate-surrogacy-in-india-nayanthara-vignesh-8202717/, for an overview of surrogacy laws in India.

11 *Id.*

12 *See* Anita L. Allen, *The Black Surrogate Mother*, 8 HARV. BLACKLETTER J. 17, 17 (1991).

13 *Id.* at 18.

14 *Id.* at 30.

## 3. ALLOWING SURROGACY RESPECTS AUTONOMY AND REPRODUCTIVE RIGHTS

Despite these critiques, advocates of surrogacy argue that surrogacy in fact respects and promotes the rights of all the parties involved. Moreover, empirical evidence in developed countries like the United States, while somewhat limited, contradicts the fears that surrogacy in developed countries involves exploitation.

Allowing and enforcing commercial surrogacy arrangements respects two crucial aspects of liberty: *autonomy* and *reproductive freedom*. First, allowing parties to enter into surrogacy arrangements respects the autonomy of each of the parties, including the surrogate, to agree to whatever arrangement they see appropriate for themselves. Second, allowing surrogacy arrangements also respects the reproductive liberty interests at stake for each of the parties to those arrangements. For the surrogate, that means using her reproductive abilities in the way that she wants. For the intended parents, it means allowing them to become parents and be genetically related to their children where they otherwise might not be able to do so.

One of the foundational principles of contract law is the autonomy of the parties to any contract to agree to whatever those parties see fit for themselves. This libertarian principle is also referred to as liberty of contract and has a long history of being respected and protected under the United States Constitution.[15]

---

[15] Lochner v. New York, 198 U.S. 45 (1905).

Going back to the landmark case of *Lochner v. New York*, the Supreme Court announced that a liberty of contract is guaranteed by the U.S. Constitution.[16] Further, individuals should be allowed the liberty to make their own chosen arrangements through contract and any government encroachment on that liberty should be evaluated critically.[17]

The *Lochner* case involved workplace regulations put in place to protect bakers in New York and the Supreme Court struck those down as being an unwarranted intrusion on the liberty of bakers and their employers to strike their own bargain.[18] The case has been widely criticized based, among other things, on the fact that the bakers were not able to actually freely bargain with their employers in that era.[19] Nonetheless, the central principle of the case, that individuals should be allowed the liberty to arrange their own affairs through contract endures.

In the surrogacy context, this principle was well articulated by the Supreme Court of Tennessee in a case decided in 2014, *In re Baby*.[20] In that case the court confronted a traditional surrogacy arrangement where the surrogate pressed for parental rights after the birth of the baby. That court explained that courts have to "respect . . . the right of

---

16 *Id.* at 53.

17 *Id.* at 53–54.

18 *Id.* at 52–53.

19 *See generally* Joseph F. Morrissey, Lochner, Lawrence, *and Liberty*, 27 GA. ST. U.L. REV. 609 (2011), for a full discussion of *Lochner*, its critiques, and liberty of contract.

20 *In re* Baby, 447 S.W.3d 807, 822 (2014).

individuals to strike their own bargains, free from unnecessary interference and with the expectation that the courts will enforce a contract between competent parties."[21] As explained, below, however, the *In re Baby* court ultimately did refuse to enforce the intentions of the parties on the basis that the arrangement was against the public policy of their state.

Courts in the United States typically do defer to the autonomy of the parties and enforce parties' agreements, except in cases where there is some defect in the contracting process or some overriding issues of public policy. One example of a defect in the parties contracting process is if there is any misrepresentation of any important part of the bargain between the parties.[22] Another example is where one of the parties exerts undue influence over the other party and effectively coerces the other party to agree to the bargain.[23] In the extreme, one party

---

[21] *Id.*

[22] For a recent example and explanation of misrepresentation in the context of surrogacy, *see* Poe v. Doe, 540 F. Supp. 3d 1193, 1195 (S.D. Fla. 2020), where the surrogate alleged that the intended parents misled her into believing the embryo transferred to her was created with the intended father's sperm. That claim was dismissed as the surrogate sought damages but couldn't show any monetary loss. *Id.* at 1198.

[23] For a classic example and explanation of undue influence, *see* Odorizzi v. Bloomfield School District, 54 Cal. Rptr. 533, 539–40 (Cal. Dist. Ct. App. 1966), where a teacher resigned after being outed as gay, and he alleged the school board superintendent and his principal exerted undue influence over him to get him to sign the resignation. The court found that the school board representatives had obtained Odorizzi's "signature but not his

might be said to be under duress and to not have freely entered into the bargain.[24] In addition, contracts that are judged to be so grossly unfair that they *shock the conscience* can be deemed by a court to be unconscionable and therefore void.[25]

Public policy is a doctrine that has evolved that specifically overrides the autonomy of the parties to enter into contractual arrangements and have those arrangements upheld. If a court decides that upholding a particular contractual arrangement would be against the public policy of that jurisdiction, then a court might well decline to enforce a contract, despite the clear intentions of the parties.

---

consent to his resignation" through their "high-pressure" tactics. *Id.* at 543.

[24] For a general example and explanation of duress, *see* Totem Marine Tug & Barge, Inc. v. Alyeska Pipeline Serv. Co., 584 P.2d 15, 19 (Alaska 1978), where a company alleged it signed a settlement agreement out of economic duress because it was facing bankruptcy. Duress was alleged in the context of surrogacy in a case where actress Sofia Vergara and her then boyfriend, Nicholas Loeb, had created embryos for use in a surrogacy arrangement and had signed a form directive concerning what to do with those embryos in the case of either Vergara or Loeb's death. *Ex rel* Human Embryo #4 HB-A v. Vergara, No. 17-1498, 2017 WL 3686569, *2 (E.D. La. Aug. 25, 2017). After the couple broke up, Loeb sought to have the form directive declared void because he claimed he signed it under duress. *Id.* The case ultimately was dismissed on other grounds. *Id.* at *7.

[25] For a classic example and explanation of unconscionability, *see* Williams v. Walker-Thomas Furniture Co., 350 F.2d 445, 447, 449–50 (D.C. Cir. 1965), where consumers who purchased furnishings agreed to a repossession clause that reached all items ever purchased from seller, contract could be unconscionable.

The public policy exception was invoked in the *Baby M* case.[26] In 1988, the New Jersey Supreme Court found that surrogacy arrangements that stipulated that the surrogate give up parental rights in advance of the birth of the child were against that expressed public policy of the state.[27] State adoption provisions did not allow a woman who gives birth to give up parental rights before the child was born.[28] Moreover, custody in situations where two parents are in a contest was to be determined by the best interests of the child and not an agreement entered into before the child was born.[29] The court referred to the surrogacy agreement as thus being "offensive to the public policy" of the state.[30] Accordingly, the court refused to enforce the clear intentions of the parties as reflected in their surrogacy agreement.[31]

The Tennessee *In re Baby* case from 2014, discussed above, also ended up finding that surrogacy was against the public policy of the state of Tennessee.[32] Accordingly, the court refused to honor the provisions of the surrogacy arrangement that provided for the traditional surrogate to give up parental rights before the birth of the baby.[33] Again, that court stressed that it ordinarily would enforce

---

26 *In re* Baby M, 537 A.2d 1227, 1238 (N.J. 1988).

27 *Id.* at 1246–1247.

28 *Id.* at 1245.

29 *Id.* at 1246.

30 *Id.*

31 *Id.* at 1244.

32 *In re* Baby, 447 S.W.3d 807, 834 (Tenn. 2014).

33 *Id.*

the intentions of the parties, but could not do so in cases where there would be a clear violation of the public policy of that state.[34] "In order to strike the proper balance between freedom of contract and competing policy interests, we have held that a contract is unenforceable on public policy grounds only when its terms clearly violate the public policy of our state."[35] The *In re Baby* court then found that a contractual agreement by a genetically related parent, the traditional surrogate, to give up parental rights ran counter to the family law statutes of Tennessee, which address relinquishing parental rights, and which require courts to consider the best interests of the child.[36]

While the *Baby M* and *In re Baby* courts allowed what they considered to be public policy concerns to prevail over the autonomy of the parties, other court decisions regarding surrogacy have reached the opposite result. *Johnson v. Calvert* is a landmark case from 1990 decided by a California court.[37] In Calvert the surrogate decided to sue for parental rights and custody of the child she carried, despite her agreement with the intended parents to give up those rights.[38]

The *Calvert* case is different from the *Baby M* and *In re Baby* cases in an important way. Both the *Baby M* and *In re Baby* cases involved traditional

---

[34] *Id.* at 822–823.

[35] *Id.*

[36] *Id.* at 834.

[37] Johnson v. Calvert, 851 P.2d 776 (Cal. 1993).

[38] *Id.* at 778.

surrogacy arrangements, where the surrogate's own egg was used in the process. *Calvert* involved a gestational surrogacy arrangement. In the *Calvert* case, the intended parents used the intended mother's egg.[39] The intended mother's uterus had been removed for medical reasons.[40] So, while the intended parents needed the help of a surrogate to carry their baby, they still were able to use their own egg and sperm.[41] Therefore, the surrogate was a gestational surrogate who was not genetically related to the baby born in any way.

In the *Calvert* case, the California court found that in that gestational surrogacy situation, the intentions of the parties as expressed in their surrogacy agreement should be honored.[42] Accordingly, the court upheld that agreement, and awarded parental rights and custody to the intended parents.[43] In its very thoughtful discussion, the *Calvert* court reasoned that gestating a baby and being the genetic-related parent are both arguments that support a claim of parenthood.[44] But, the court reasoned, where the intentions of the intended parents were the driving force behind the creation of the child, and where awarding custody to the intended parents would be in line with the interests

---

39 *Id.*

40 *Id.*

41 *Id.*

42 *Id.* at 782.

43 *Id.*

44 *Id.*

of the child, parental rights should vest in accord with the expressed intention of the parties.[45]

While the law on surrogacy in the United States still does vary state by state, the trend has been for courts and statutes in the United States to follow the *Calvert* court and enforce the intentions of the parties to a gestational surrogacy arrangement. (See Chapter 6 for an overview of the laws of each of the states.) Statutes like the Illinois Gestational Surrogacy Act provide that gestational surrogacy arrangements are enforceable.[46]

| **Gestational Versus Traditional Surrogacy** |
| --- |
| As the cases and statutes show, the distinction between gestational and traditional surrogacy is still vitally important. Gestational surrogacy arrangements are far more likely to be upheld and enforced since the surrogate is not genetically related to the child or children she births. |

Other cases have tended to follow the *Calvert* case when gestational surrogacy is involved. A relatively recent case out of Iowa did just that.[47] The Iowa Supreme Court held in 2018 that a gestational surrogacy contract was enforceable under the laws of Iowa.[48] That court reasoned that enforcement was the only way to give effect to the intentions of all of

---

[45] *Id.* at 783.

[46] *See* Gestational Surrogacy Act, 750 ILL. COMP. STAT. ANN. 47 (West 2023).

[47] P.M. v. T.B., 907 N.W.2d 522, 543 (Iowa 2018).

[48] *Id.* at 540.

the parties, and to honor the autonomy of any surrogate to agree to participate in such an arrangement.[49]

| **Review the Laws of Your Jurisdiction** |
| --- |
| Before proceeding with a surrogacy arrangement, be sure to review the laws of your jurisdiction. If you are still living in a jurisdiction that does not support and enforce even gestational surrogacy arrangements, you will want to consider proceeding in a jurisdiction that does. See *Chapter 4: Managing the Law to Minimize Your Risk*. |

Beyond respecting the autonomy of the parties, enforcing a surrogacy arrangement also respects the reproductive liberty interests of all the parties to the arrangement. Even in the early years when surrogacy became viable and many women's rights advocates were skeptical of the arrangements, there were women's advocates that supported commercial surrogacy on the basis of this reproductive liberty interest.[50]

*Roe v. Wade* was the landmark decision from 1973 that held that women should have the right to choose to have an abortion in certain time frames and with

---

49 *Id.* at 525.

50 Lori B. Andrews, *Surrogacy Motherhood: The Challenge for Feminists*, 16 L. Med. & Health Care 72, 72 (1988), https://www.cambridge.org/core/journals/law-medicine-and-healthcare/article/abs/surrogate-motherhood-the-challenge-for-feminists/B229E96E946994E32B40AF2059305140.

certain conditions.[51] Some advocates then argued that to be consistent, feminists should support reproductive freedom for women more generally, whether that means the right to choose to have an abortion, or the right to choose to be a surrogate.[52]

Moreover, reproductive freedom includes not only the reproductive freedom of women to act as surrogates if they so choose, but also the reproductive liberty of intended parents who cannot become parents to genetically related children without surrogacy. Feminist advocates who are concerned about women who act as surrogates being exploited have to balance that concern with concern for these intended parents.[53]

Intended parents involved with surrogacy are often traditional, opposite-sex married couples, but increasingly intended parents are single men or women or same-sex male couples, married or unmarried.[54] Feminist advocates have generally supported equality for all kinds of diverse families and strived to "free people in society from constricting gender roles."[55] So, despite the fears of exploitation involved with surrogacy, allowing single people and same-sex couples to form families through surrogacy is, in fact, supporting that feminist goal.

---

[51] Roe v. Wade, 410 U.S. 113, 164–65 (1973). Note that almost 50 years later in 2022, *Roe v. Wade* was overturned in Dobbs v. Jackson Women's Health Organization, 597 U.S. 215 (2022).

[52] Andrews, *supra* note 50, at 73.

[53] Ainsworth, *supra* note 7, at 1091.

[54] *See id.*

[55] *Id.*

## 4. EMPIRICAL STUDIES SHOW NO EXPLOITATION

After several decades of commercial surrogacy growing in popularity in the United States there are some empirical studies that are at odds with exploitation fears and concerns. One prominent scholar and law professor, Professor Lori Andrews, did a survey of over 80 surrogates and intended parents in the late 1980s.[56] Andrews confessed that she went into the project with a bias, expecting to find that at least some of the women she would meet and interview would have been exploited in some way.[57]

In a very humorous note, Andrews complained that the first surrogate she met was a healthcare professional who earned more than she did.[58] She didn't find any evidence of exploitation at all.[59] After many interviews and no evidence of exploitation, Andrews did come upon a Mexican-American woman who had been a surrogate and who seemed to be struggling financially.[60] Andrews thought she had found someone who was being forced by her circumstances to become a surrogate.[61] But again,

---

56 Lori B. Andrews, *Beyond Doctrinal Boundaries: A Legal Framework for Surrogate Motherhood*, 81 VA. L. REV. 2343, 2349 (1995).

57 *Id.*

58 *Id.*

59 *Id.* at 2350.

60 *Id.* at 2349.

61 *Id.*

that woman in fact explained that it was her pleasure to help another family have children.[62]

Another empirical study, this one published in 2010 by a Canadian law professor, Professor Karen Busby, and her student, Delaney Vun, pointed to the same conclusion, that women who had been surrogates in developed economies like the United States did not experience exploitation.[63] On the contrary, those women routinely said that they were acting out of a desire to help someone else achieve their dream of forming a family, and that they were not providing surrogacy services out of economic necessity.[64] The Busby and Vun Study was quite extensive and aggregated data from almost 40 separate empirical studies of women who had been surrogates.[65]

The Busby and Vun Study concluded that "the empirical research establishes that surrogate mothers are mature, experienced, stable, self-aware, and extroverted non-conformists who make the initial decision that surrogacy is something that they want to do."[66] Moreover, surrogates reported that they were generally comfortable giving custody of any baby born to the intended parents and never

---

62 *Id.* at 2350.

63 Busby & Vun, *supra* note 4, at 80.

64 *Id.*

65 *Id.* at 39.

66 *Id.* at 52.

considered the child or children born to the be their own.[67]

Interestingly, the Busby and Vun Study found that the surrogates who were most satisfied with their experiences were the ones with a positive relationship with the intended parent or parents.[68] That fact underscores how important it is for a surrogate to make sure she works with an intended parent or intended parents who are the right fit for her. Initial discussions and contract negotiations can help surrogates figure out if the fit is right, or if, for example, the intended parent or parents might be too aggressive or controlling.

Another scholar focusing on empirical work, Lina Peng, pointed out that by 2014 it was difficult to substantiate the fears that there would be significant harm to women in the United States who acted as surrogates.[69] Instead, she found that "in the vast majority of surrogacy arrangements, surrogate mothers have positive experiences, have no issues relinquishing the child, and want to be surrogates again."[70]

---

[67] *Id.* at 73.

[68] *Id.* at 72.

[69] Lina Peng, *Surrogate Mothers: An Exploration of the Empirical and the Normative*, 21 J. GENDER, SOC. POL'Y & LAW 555, 560 (2014), https://digitalcommons.wcl.american.edu/cgi/viewcontent.cgi?article=1610&context=jgspl; *See also* Elly Teman, *The Social Construction of Surrogacy Research: An Anthropological Critique of the Psychosocial Scholarship on Surrogate Motherhood*, 67 SOC. SCI. & MED. 1104, 1104 (2008).

[70] Peng, *supra* note 69, at 556.

These empirical studies coincide perfectly with our own experience with our surrogate and the surrogates we have met. Those surrogates have been very happy with their experience. They all have said that finances were not the main reason they wanted to be a surrogate, but that instead they wanted to help others achieve their dream of forming a family. They had no trouble waiving parental rights and giving custody of the child or children born to their intended parents. Moreover, those surrogates continue to have a strong and positive relationship with those intended parents and the children they helped bring into this world.

## 5. ENSURING A POSITIVE SURROGACY EXPERIENCE

If you are considering being a surrogate, consider the arguments that women's advocates have made, but also consider your own intentions and motivations. If surrogacy seems like it's right for you, you can take steps to make sure your experience is positive.

Try to make sure you can form a strong and healthy relationship with your intended parent or parents. You can make that assessment during your first meetings and throughout your discussions of the surrogacy agreement. Don't feel confined to only interact with the intended parent(s) on their terms or the terms of any agency you might have.

Invite the intended parent(s) to have lunch or dinner, or even just take a walk together. Talk to them about their family formation goals, and how they expect to parent. Address issues early on that might be important to you like how much involvement they expect to have in the pregnancy. Do you want them to call or visit regularly during the pregnancy, or would you prefer to limit their involvement to doctor's appointments? What sort of behavioral restrictions would they like for their surrogate? Some intended parents want to be involved in everything the surrogate does during pregnancy, including what the surrogate has for her meals. That might be too much for you. All of these questions can help both you and the intended parent or parents assess whether you should be working together. Just because you have begun the process with a particular intended parent or parents does not mean you have to agree to continue to work with those people, especially if you have not yet signed the surrogacy agreement.

Surrogacy statutes generally stipulate that a surrogate be represented by independent counsel in negotiating a surrogacy arrangement. The intended parent or parents should pay the fees for that representation. Even if the governing statute does not require it, you should request to have an attorney represent you as the surrogate.

Attorneys acting for you as a surrogate are meant to safeguard you from any kind of exploitation that the critics have feared might occur. Those attorneys are meant to ensure that there are no defects in the contracting process of agreeing to the surrogacy arrangement. There is no fraud, no coercion of any sort, and certainly no resulting bargain that would be grossly unfair or unconscionable.

Moreover, the attorney is meant to ensure that the surrogate understands her commitments, and freely and fairly agrees to enter into the arrangement. Be sure to use that attorney wisely. Ask all the questions you have. Don't be shy. The attorney likely will have heard the questions before and be able to provide answers.

Never agree to anything you don't understand. And don't agree to anything that makes you uncomfortable, including any behavioral restrictions that might be discussed and, in particular, any unwanted control over your own medical decisions. If the intended parents are not comfortable with your boundaries, you are probably better off working with others.

**Ensuring a Positive Surrogacy Experience**

If you have considered the criticisms of surrogacy and still think that being a surrogate is right for you, take steps to try to ensure you have the best experience possible, including:

1. **Find the right intended parent(s)**—Try to make sure the intended parent(s) you are considering working with are the right fit for you. Early but meaningful conversations about the surrogacy arrangement will help you make that decision.

2. **Review the surrogacy agreement**—Read the draft of the surrogacy agreement carefully. Highlight any issues or questions you have or anything that makes you even slightly uncomfortable.
3. **Consult with your attorney**—Be sure to use the attorney provided to you to resolve any issues or questions you have with the surrogacy agreement. If the intended parent(s) are not willing to accept what you are comfortable with, then you are likely better off working with others.

If a surrogate enters into an arrangement carefully and with good counsel from her advisors, there is every reason to expect the experience to be just like the one that so many other surrogates have had. Lori Andrews concluded from her empirical study that women who chose to become surrogates got a "tremendous psychic benefit[ ]" from being able to help others achieve their joyous goal of family formation.[71] "Many viewed themselves as feminists who were exercising reproductive choice and demonstrating an ethic of care."[72] It is my hope that if you choose to become a surrogate, you have an equally empowering and uplifting experience.

[71] Andrews, *supra* note 56, at 2354.

[72] *Id.*

# CHAPTER 4

# MANAGING THE LAW TO MINIMIZE YOUR RISK

Just as every country in the world has its own laws affecting surrogacy, so too each state in the United States has different laws regarding surrogacy. This chapter will discuss how to manage those laws to minimize the risk to the intended parents that their surrogacy arrangement will not be upheld. Throughout the discussion, for convenience I will refer to the intended parents, but please know that I mean to include a single intended parent as well.

## 1. STRUCTURE THE ARRANGEMENT TO MINIMIZE RISK

It will be the intended parents who structure the surrogacy arrangement. So, it is largely up to the intended parents to structure their arrangement in a way that maximizes the chances that the arrangement will be supported and enforced under the relevant laws. If a surrogacy arrangement is not upheld under the relevant laws, intended parents risk a surrogate changing her mind and attempting to keep custody and establish her own parental rights over any child born. That was the situation in the *Baby M* and *In re Baby* cases discussed in Chapters 2 and 3.

But managing the laws is also important for surrogates who should be aware of these decisions as well and seek to ensure that the arrangement takes place under surrogacy supportive laws. For a surrogate, if a surrogacy agreement is not upheld, intended parents might decide not to take parental rights and custody of the child born and the surrogate might feel compelled to raise the child herself. These cases have actually occurred as, for example, in the case where the child is found to have significant developmental or medical challenges and the intended parents make the decision that they don't want to raise such a child.[1]

**Tales from the Field: Legal Risks for Surrogates**

It's easy to think of the risks for intended parents of a surrogate trying to exert parental rights over a child born. In some cases, however, the intended parents end up not wanting to take parental responsibility for any child born from the surrogacy arrangement. That leaves the surrogate faced with either accepting parental responsibility or finding an adoptive home for any children born.In a case like that where the surrogate had twins, the intended parents had split up and were getting a divorce.[2] At that point they did not want

---

[1] For a discussion of intended parents reneging on their obligations after a pregnancy is well underway, *see* Katherine Drabiak, *Infants Born Through Surrogacy Contracts Cannot Be Canceled or Returned*, PETRIE-FLOM CTR. AT HARV. L. SCH.: BILL OF HEALTH (Feb. 8, 2021), https://blog.petrieflom.law.harvard.edu/2021/02/08/surrogacy-contracts-canceled/.

[2] For details on this story, *see* Caitlin Keating, *Parents Shockingly Back Out on Surrogate Mom Pregnant with Twins: "It's Your Problem Now,"* PEOPLE MAG., Mar. 4, 2016, https://www.yahoo.com/entertainment/parents-shockingly-back-surrogate-mom-200638733.html.

the twins the surrogate was carrying for them. The surrogate had even gone through a selective reduction when she found she was actually pregnant with triplets. Faced with the possibility of having to raise twins as a single mom who already had a daughter, the surrogate took legal action against the intended parents. Those intended parents ultimately agreed to give up all parental rights so that the twins born could be adopted by a good family that did want them.

If the surrogacy laws in the state of the intended parents and/or their surrogate will support and enforce a surrogacy arrangement, then the intended parents should proceed in that state, including working with a surrogate there and having their baby born there. The parties should expressly agree that the laws of that state will apply to their arrangement. The parties then need only follow that law and its requirements.

If, however, the law in the intended parents' state or the state of the chosen surrogate does not permit a surrogacy arrangement, or will not enforce a surrogacy agreement, then intended parents have two potential options. Keep in mind that the state where the child is born is most likely to be the state where a custody battle would occur.

The first, and typically better option is to proceed by having the surrogate give birth in a state that does support and enforce surrogacy arrangements. That may simply mean choosing to work with a surrogate who lives in a surrogacy supportive state. In that case, the parties should also expressly agree that the laws of that state will apply to their arrangement. This is the safest approach. The baby will be born in the surrogacy supportive state and all the parties will have agreed that the laws of that state should govern. So, if there are any legal challenges to the arrangement, the parties' intentions as outlined in the surrogacy agreement should be honored and enforced.

A second, riskier option is to proceed in the state where the intended parents and/or the surrogate live, but use a choice of law provision to choose the laws of a surrogacy supportive state to govern the agreement. This second option is the much riskier of the two options. State courts tend to honor such choice of law provisions, but not if they perceive them to contravene the public policy of the state whose law would otherwise apply.[3] Sometimes courts do not honor choice of law clauses if the state whose law was chosen does not have a substantial connection to the subject of the contract—in this case the surrogacy arrangement. This chapter will examine each of these options in turn.

---

[3] Sonia Bychkov Green, *Interstate Intercourse: How Modern Assisted Reproductive Technologies Challenge the Traditional Realm of Conflicts of Law*, 24 WIS. J.L. GENDER & SOC'Y 25, 90 (2009).

### Choosing the Law to Manage Your Risks

Because the laws regarding surrogacy are different in all the states in the United States, parties should strive to ensure that their arrangement is governed by the laws of a surrogacy supportive state. ***Be sure to work with your attorney on managing these risks*** and choosing the best possible option for you.

1. Proceed physically in a surrogacy supportive state and have the law of that state expressly identified in the surrogacy agreement as controlling—this is generally the **best option** because it is the least risky. If the surrogate lives in and gives birth in a surrogacy supportive state, and the parties agreed to be bound by the laws of that state, then the intentions of the parties as set forth in their agreement should be honored.
2. If proceeding in a surrogacy supportive state is not feasible, then expressly choose to have the laws of a surrogacy supportive state govern the surrogacy arrangement, but have as many meaningful contacts with the chosen state as possible to maximize the chances of that choice of law being upheld. But beware of this option as some courts will not enforce a choice of law that the court deems undermines the public policy of their own state.

## 2. PROCEED IN A STATE WHERE SURROGACY IS SUPPORTED

If the intended parents' home state does not support surrogacy, then they should proceed physically in a state that does. By doing this, the intended parent can reduce the risk that the surrogacy arrangement would not be enforced. The states that allow and enforce surrogacy arrangements typically have the infrastructure, clinics, and agencies that specialize in surrogacy to help intended parents embark on a surrogacy arrangement at a distance.

For example, if the intended parent or parents live in Michigan, the laws of that state criminalize entering into surrogacy arrangements. Those intended parents should choose to proceed in a surrogacy supportive state. Nearby Illinois has a surrogacy law requiring courts to enforce gestational surrogacy arrangements that comply with the statute.[4] California is another jurisdiction where gestational surrogacy agreements have long been enforced by courts.[5] California also now has a

---

[4] *See infra* Chapter 5. *See also* 750 ILL. COMP. STAT. ANN. 47/25 (West 2023).

[5] *See, e.g.*, Johnson v. Calvert, 851 P.2d 776 (Cal. 1993) (enforcing a gestational surrogacy agreement). *Calvert* was discussed in Chapter 3. In *Calvert*, the court held that the intended parents in a gestational surrogacy agreement should be recognized as the natural and legal parents. *Id.* at 782. The court decided that the person who intended to procreate, in this case that was the mother who provided her egg to the surrogate, should be considered the natural mother. *Id. See also* Tamar Lewin, *Surrogates and Couples Face a Maze of Laws, State by State*, N.Y. TIMES (Sept. 17, 2014), https://www.nytimes.com/2014/09/18/us/

surrogacy statute, which enforces the intentions of the parties to any surrogacy arrangement that complies with the statute.[6]

As Chapter 6 sets forth, more and more of the states in the United States now support and enforce surrogacy arrangements. So, it is easier than ever for an intended parent or parents to find a surrogacy supportive jurisdiction that is convenient.

Intended parents should also survey the clinics and agencies (if they choose to use one) that may work within each of the jurisdictions. If intended parents are going to proceed in a state other than the one where they live, it is more likely that they will need the help of an agency to find their surrogate in that state. Intended parents should find a clinic and an agency that they are comfortable with in a surrogacy supportive state that is convenient for them.

Ultimately, intended parents should choose a state that supports surrogacy agreements and then conduct most, if not all, of the actions related to their surrogacy arrangement in that state. The child's place of the birth is likely to be the jurisdiction where any custody battle would occur and where it is crucial for the applicable law to support surrogacy.[7]

---

surrogates-and-couples-face-a-maze-of-laws-state-by-state.html (describing California as having the "most permissive law" and "a booming surrogacy industry" as a result).

[6] *See* CAL. FAM. CODE § 7962(i) (West 2023).

[7] UNIF. CHILD CUSTODY JURISDICTION & ENF'T ACT § 201 (UNIF. L. COMM'N 1997), https://www.uniformlaws.org/HigherLogic/System/DownloadDocumentFile.ashx?Document

Intended parents should also make sure all relevant agreements are governed by the law of that surrogacy supportive state. In contract-related disputes, if the parties do not use a choice of law provision in their agreements, then it is still likely that the law of the state where they proceed will apply simply based on general choice of law rules.[8]

It is always best to be clear in the agreements so that there is no doubt. If the intended parents specify the law of the surrogacy supportive state where they are going to proceed and they in fact do proceed there, then there should be little risk of any other law being applied. After the surrogate successfully delivers a child or children for the intended parents, the

---

FileKey=ec72931d-d12b-ef73-8986-9407ff85c529&forceDialog=0. Under § 201 of this Act, the child's home state is the state with jurisdiction to make the initial child-custody determinations. *Id.* The Act defines the *Home State* for a child who is less than six months old as the state in which the child lived from birth. *Id.* at § 102(7). *See generally*, Jessica Grose, *The Sherri Shepherd Surrogacy Case Is a Mess,* SLATE (Apr. 28, 2015, 5:54 PM), http://www.slate.com/blogs/xx_factor/2015/04/28/sherri_shepherd_surrogacy_case_there_s_little_consensus_on_the_ethical_dimensions.html (discussing the complex nature of surrogacy law in the United States).

[8] The common law doctrine of *lex loci contractus* requires that, when determining the construction, validity, enforceability, or interpretation of a contract, the court applies the law of the jurisdiction where the contract was made. *See, e.g.*, Cunningham v. Feinberg, 107 A.3d 1194, 1204–05 (Md. 2015) (discussing common law choice of law rules in contracts.). *See generally* Susan Frelich Appleton, *Surrogacy Arrangements and the Conflict of Laws,* 1990 WIS. L. REV. 399, 413 (1990) (discussing the fact that choice of law analysis will apply to contractual claims and noting that the contract's enforceability may be subsumed by the question of whether the court will grant an adoption, if necessary, in a surrogacy case).

intended parents will need to assert their parental rights in that state, and they will want the courts of that state to apply their laws to the surrogacy arrangement.

Managing a surrogacy arrangement at a distance involves more costs and potentially more effort since every appointment will involve either travel or discussions over the phone or internet. Still, the risks of a surrogacy arrangement going sour and having the relevant courts not support the intentions of the parties and enforce the agreement are too great to ignore.

As shown with the *Baby M* and *In re Baby* cases, discussed in Chapters 2 and 3, surrogates do sometimes decide that they want to keep custody of the child or children born.[9] If a surrogacy agreement is not enforced, then the surrogate may indeed have a chance to get parental rights over the child.[10] If a surrogate does win parental rights over a child born but the intended father is also the genetic father, then the intended father may end up without custody but may still have to pay child support to the surrogate. Intended parents should be careful to avoid this awful scenario by proceeding in a jurisdiction that supports surrogacy.

Managing the law is all about managing risk. In fact, most surrogacy arrangements do not end up in

---

9 *See In re* Baby M, 537 A.2d 1227, 1236 (N.J. 1988); *In re* Baby, 447 S.W.3d 807, 816 (Tenn. 2014).

10 *In re Baby M*, 537 A.2d at 1243–1244; *In re Baby*, 447 S.W.3d at 827.

court, and the parties may not have any problems even if they do proceed in a jurisdiction that does not clearly support surrogacy.

Even if the surrogate does contest custody and the intended parents' state will not enforce the surrogacy agreement, the intended parents may well still be awarded full custody if it is in the best interests of the child. This was the end result in both the *Baby M* and the *In re Baby* cases.[11] If intended parents proceed with gestational surrogacy (where the surrogate is not the genetic parent), then custody may well be awarded to the intended parents because at least one of them is a genetic parent.[12]

As a result, while not advisable, intended parents still might take the risk of proceeding in their home state—even if the state that does not clearly support their surrogacy arrangement. Again, if the intended parents do live in one of the states where surrogacy is not supported, then they should consult an attorney to get specific advice on how to manage the legal risks.

---

[11] *In re Baby M*, 537 A.2d at 1259; *In re Baby*, 447 S.W.3d at 833.

[12] *See, e.g.*, Gray v. Chambers, 634 N.Y.S.2d 864, 865 (N.Y. App. Div. 1995) (citations omitted) ("It is fundamental that a biological parent has a claim of custody of his or her child, superior to that of all others, in the absence of surrender, abandonment, persistent neglect, unfitness, disruption of custody over an extended period of time or other extraordinary circumstances. Until it is shown that one of these circumstances exists, the inquiry is at an end and the biological parent must be given custody of the child.").

## 3. ALTERNATIVELY, PROCEED UNDER THE LAWS OF A SURROGACY SUPPORTIVE STATE

If physically proceeding in a state other than the one where the intended parents and/or surrogate live seems daunting, or if the intended parents really want to work with a surrogate who lives in their home state, then an alternative option is to add a choice of law clause to the surrogacy agreement that uses the law of a surrogacy supportive state to govern the agreement. In this situation, a court may apply the law of that pro-surrogacy state if there are any challenges to the agreement. But proceed with caution and consult your attorney before choosing this option. Consider the following case study.

## 4. CHOICE OF LAW CASE STUDY: *IN RE BABY BOY A*

The *Baby M* case from the 1980s discussed in Chapter 2 has a dizzying array of facts that highlight some of the risks associated with surrogacy. Another much more recent case from 2007, *In re Baby Boy A.*, is quite possibly even more horrific for an intended parent.

Although *Baby Boy A* is much more recent than the *Baby M* case, it has a similar fact pattern. In both cases the surrogate decided to keep custody of the child after the child was born, despite having entered into a surrogacy agreement where she agreed to give custody to the intended father.

The facts of the *Baby Boy A* case are even more outrageous than the facts of *Baby M.* In *Baby Boy A*, a single gay man, J.M.A., sought to have a biological child with the help of a surrogate.[13] The intended parent, J.M.A., lived in New York City. He asked his sister Mary, who lived in Minnesota, to be his surrogate. She declined but brought the idea up to her adult daughter, J.M.A.'s niece, who also lived in Minnesota. The niece then contacted J.M.A. and volunteered to be his surrogate. At that time, the niece was currently pregnant, and the parties agreed to wait until after the niece had her baby before deciding on anything definitively.

The niece had her baby, and continued to express an interest in being a surrogate for J.M.A. She and J.M.A. executed a gestational surrogacy agreement where she agreed to give custody of any child born to J.M.A.[14] The parties also agreed that J.M.A. would reimburse all expenses and pay the niece $20,000 in compensation.

Partway through the pregnancy the nightmare began for J.M.A. His niece contacted him and demanded an additional $120,000 in compensation.[15] She told J.M.A. that she actually would abort the child if he did not pay the additional sum of money.

It is so hard to imagine someone who began a surrogacy relationship with seemingly the best of

---

[13] Baby Boy A. v. J.M.A., No. A07-452, 2007 WL 4304448, at *1 (Minn. Ct. App. Dec. 11, 2007).

[14] *Id.*

[15] *Id.* at *2.

intentions then being so cruel. In some ways, this was a case of extortion. In other ways, it was like a kidnapping with a threat of murder if the ransom was not paid.

Faced with this unbelievable demand, J.M.A. refused to negotiate or pay. Thankfully for J.M.A., the surrogate niece did not go through with the abortion, and she did give birth to a healthy child. However, the surrogate niece also decided to name the child, and attempted to retain all parental and custody rights over the child. It was at this point that J.M.A. brought suit in the courts of Minnesota to assert his parental rights and to obtain custody of the child.[16]

J.M.A. and his niece's surrogacy agreement included a choice of law clause that used the laws of Illinois to govern the agreement. The Minnesota state court evaluated the surrogacy agreement and its choice of law clause.[17] In an unpublished opinion, the Minnesota court decided to honor the Illinois choice of law and thus enforced the surrogacy agreement.[18]

The court evaluated the choice of law clause and explained that surrogacy agreements with choice of law clauses that are freely entered into by the parties are enforceable unless they are a bad-faith attempt to evade Minnesota law.[19] Since there was no

---

16 *Id.* at *2.

17 *Id.* at *3.

18 *Id.*

19 *Id.*

Minnesota law regarding surrogacy (and there still is none), the court found no attempt by the parties to evade Minnesota law. The court applied Illinois law to the gestational surrogacy agreement.[20]

Since Minnesota had no law expressly addressing surrogacy, it was smart for the intended parent in *In re Baby Boy A* to include the Illinois choice of law clause. The Minnesota courts hearing the matter upheld that choice of law clause, applied Illinois law, and enforced the surrogacy agreement.[21] J.M.A. was determined to be the father, and he was given custody of the child.

Unfortunately, this case was not reported by the court, which means that the court's decision is not precedent for Minnesota courts.[22] But despite the case's lack of precedential value, the case's facts are instructive. First, it is an example of a case where a court did uphold the parties' choice of law clause. Second, it illustrates that even surrogacy agreements between relatives can derail. In this respect, parties should put legal protections in place in advance to protect the interests of the intended parent, regardless of how much they trust their surrogate.

While choice of law standards are different in each state, courts in all states will generally respect the choice of law provisions adopted by the parties to a contract.[23] However, as in the *Baby Boy A* case, many

---

20 *Id.* at *8.

21 *Id.* at *7.

22 MINN. STAT. ANN. § 480A.08(3)(b) (West 2023).

23 *See* Green, *supra* note 3, at 90.

state courts will not enforce choice of law provisions if the court believes that the parties are acting in bad faith or trying to evade the laws or policies of the state in which the court sits.[24]

In Florida, for example, the courts have stated that choice of law clauses should be honored "unless a showing is made that the law of the chosen forum contravenes strong public policy or that the clause is otherwise unreasonable or unjust."[25] In one recent surrogacy case in Florida heard by a federal court, the court reiterated that principle, "Under Florida law, courts will enforce 'choice of law provisions unless the law of the chosen forum contravenes strong public policy.' "[26] Without any challenge to the choice of law in that case, that court applied the parties' chosen law, Tennessee law, to their surrogacy arrangement. Current Tennessee law appears to support surrogacy arrangements.

Choice of law standards are problematic for parties who want their surrogacy agreement to be governed by the laws of a surrogacy supportive state but who proceed in a state that does not support surrogacy. Choosing the laws of a pro-surrogacy state may be found to be against the public policy of the state considering the case. Thus, parties in those states should strongly consider proceeding with as many

---

[24] *Baby Boy A.*, 2007 WL 4304448 at *3.

[25] Magner Int'l Corp. v. Brett, 960 So. 2d 841, 843–844 (Fla. Dist. Ct. App. 2007).

[26] Poe v. Doe 540 F.Supp. 3d 1193, 1196 (S.D. Fla. 2020) (citing Maxcess, Inc. v. Lucent Techs., Inc., 433 F.3d 1337, 1341 (11th Cir. 2005)).

connections as possible to a surrogacy supportive state. The least risky approach would be to work with a surrogate in a surrogacy supportive state.

But even if intended parents want to work with a surrogate in their home state and their home state is not supportive of surrogacy, the intended parents can still strive to ensure that there are contacts with a surrogacy supportive state. Perhaps the surrogacy agency, fertility clinic, or egg donor is in that other state, or maybe the parties meet, negotiate, and sign their surrogacy agreement in that other state.

Many state courts will look to these kinds of contacts between the parties to the contract and the jurisdiction of the applicable governing law before enforcing that choice of law. In the *Baby Boy A* case, for example, the parties actually used an IVF clinic in Illinois and signed a variety of documents in Illinois.[27] While the Minnesota court did not rely on these connections in order to enforce the Illinois choice of law, it did mention those facts in its opinion.[28]

But other states, including California, expressly evaluate whether the law chosen bears a "substantial relationship" to the transaction involved.[29] If there is

---

[27] *Baby Boy A.*, 2007 WL 4304448 at *2.

[28] *Id.*

[29] *See, e.g.*, Nedlloyd Lines B.V. v. Superior Court, 834 P.2d 1148, 1151–1152 (Cal. 1992); *see generally*, RESTATEMENT (SECOND) OF CONFLICTS OF LAWS § 187 (1971) (stating that the parties' contractual choice of law will be applied unless "the chosen state has no substantial relationship to the parties or the

no such relationship, then courts may not honor the choice of law provision. Because some courts will look for a connection to the jurisdiction chosen for the applicable law, the safest approach is to do something substantial in connection with the surrogacy arrangement in that state beyond just choosing its law. As with proceeding physically in that state, this may include using a clinic in that state, or using an agency, surrogate, or egg donor from that state.

This area of law is complicated. It is strongly recommended that parties proceed physically in a surrogacy supportive state and expressly agree in their contracts that the laws of that state govern their surrogacy arrangement. If that doesn't make sense for the parties to a particular surrogacy arrangement, then choosing to be governed by the laws of a surrogacy supportive state and trying to create as many contacts with that state as possible is an alternative, albeit somewhat risky. Once again, parties should absolutely discuss these issues with their attorney to make sure they are proceeding prudently to manage their legal risks.

---

transaction and there is no other reasonable basis for the parties' choice," or the chosen law is "contrary to a fundamental policy.").

# CHAPTER 5

# THE ILLINOIS SURROGACY ACT, AS AN EXAMPLE

As just discussed, one important way to manage legal risk is to make sure that the surrogacy arrangement is governed by the law of a surrogacy supportive state. But even then, it is important to review and understand the law that will govern the arrangement.

Generally speaking, modern surrogacy laws were drafted with the criticisms of surrogacy in mind. Recall the three specific criticisms of surrogacy explored in Chapter 3: (i) that surrogates might have a difficult time meaningfully consenting to the arrangement, and that surrogates might be (ii) exploited or (iii) commodified.

But likewise, as we have seen in the *Baby Boy A* case, surrogates might also attempt to take advantage of intended parents who ardently want to form a family. Specifically, surrogacy laws have been designed to protect each of the parties against these possibilities for abuse. Legal requirements as simple as making sure that each of the parties are represented by independent attorneys help make sure that each of the parties is able to participate in jointly structuring the surrogacy arrangement in a mutually satisfactory way.

This chapter will explore the Gestational Surrogacy Act of Illinois (the Illinois GSA), a surrogacy supportive law that went into effect in

2005.[1] While it has its critics, the GSA in many ways reflects best practices in structuring a surrogacy arrangement, including many specific protections for each of the parties to the arrangement.[2]

Other surrogacy supportive state laws contain similar provisions. For example, California's surrogacy act, which went into effect in 2013, contains several of the same kinds of important protections contained in the Illinois GSA.[3] The Illinois GSA, however, is more detailed than the California surrogacy act in its insistence upon certain safeguards for all the parties. As set forth below, those safeguards include, for example, mandatory medical and mental health consultations for all parties.[4]

Importantly, the Illinois GSA (like the California surrogacy act) is designed to be non-discriminatory. Intended parents can be any "person or persons," married or unmarried who manifests an intent to become a parent.[5] By that definition, there is apparently no restriction on who can become an intended parent.

---

1 Gestational Surrogacy Act, 750 ILL. COMP. STAT. ANN. 47 (West 2023) [hereinafter GSA].

2 Paul G. Arshagouni, *Be Fruitful and Multiply, by Other Means, if Necessary: The Time Has Come to Recognize and Enforce Gestational Surrogacy Agreements*, 61 DEPAUL L. REV. 799, 811. "With some modifications, [the Illinois GSA] can serve as a good model for future legislation." *Id.*

3 *Compare* CAL. FAM. CODE § 7962 (West 2023), *with* GSA, *supra* note 1.

4 GSA, *supra* note 1, at § 20(a)(3)–(4).

5 *Id.* at § 10.

By contrast, some states, like Florida, provide that surrogacy arrangements are only binding if the intended parents are married.[6] When the Florida surrogacy statute was adopted, gay people could not be married in Florida and so categorically were also precluded from entering into binding surrogacy arrangements. Unmarried couples and single people are still excluded.

The purpose of the Illinois GSA is set forth in the statute itself. "The purpose of this Act is to establish consistent standards and procedural safeguards for the protection of all parties involved in a gestational surrogacy contract in this State and to confirm the legal status of children born as a result of these contracts."[7]

The Illinois GSA makes clear that the intended parent or parents are the parents of the child born to a surrogate "immediately upon the birth of the child."[8] The statute also prohibits the surrogate and her husband from being considered the parents of the children.[9]

The Act has strict requirements for who can be a surrogate and for what the intended parents must do in order to qualify for the protection of the statute.[10]

---

6 FLA. STAT. ANN. § 742.15(1) (West 2023).

7 GSA, *supra* note 1, at § 5.

8 *Id.* at § 15(b)(1)–(6).

9 *Id.* at § 15(b)(6).

10 *Id.* at § 20(a)–(b).

**Requirements for the Surrogate**[11]

The Act requires that the surrogate:

1. Is at least 21 years old;
2. Has given birth to at least one child;
3. Has completed a medical evaluation;
4. Has completed a mental health evaluation;
5. Has had an independent attorney consult with her on the surrogacy agreement; and
6. Has health insurance covering her throughout the pregnancy and 8 weeks thereafter.

Each of these requirements reflects best practices for a successful surrogacy arrangement.[12] It is crucial that the surrogate is old enough to fully understand what she is doing. If the surrogate has given birth before, then the surrogate knows how her body reacts to a pregnancy. Because she will also understand the emotional ties that develop during pregnancy, she will understand the implications of carrying a child and giving custody to the intended parents. In addition, if a surrogate has her own child or children, then it may also make it less likely that she will want custody of the child or children born through the surrogacy.

It is also essential for the surrogate to be healthy and physically able to become a surrogate. Moreover,

---

[11] *Id.* at § 20(a)(1)–(6).

[12] Arshagouni, *supra* note 2, at 809–11.

it is helpful for the surrogate to undergo a mental-health consultation to establish that the surrogate is mature and stable enough to honor her commitment.

A surrogacy arrangement is complicated. Because of this, it is important that the surrogate have her own attorney. The right of the surrogate to use an attorney is an important safeguard against any exploitation of the surrogate that might otherwise occur. The surrogate's attorney will act as her advocate to help make sure that the surrogate understands all of the terms and commitments set forth in that agreement. Some of the crucial terms for the surrogate include how and when she is to be compensated, under what circumstances she may be able to terminate the pregnancy, and her commitment to support the parental rights of the intended parents. The surrogate's attorney should also help her negotiate for better, or simply more preferable, terms for herself.

Finally, the Act requires insurance coverage. The insurance will cover any major medical expenses of the surrogate throughout the pregnancy and eight weeks after birth.[13] Note that many standard insurance policies will not cover expenses related to a surrogacy. There are special policies specifically designed to cover the major medical expenses of a surrogate throughout her pregnancy. The Act states that the intended parents may purchase the

---

13 GSA, *supra* note 1, at § 20(a)(6).

insurance policy for the surrogate.[14] Insurance is discussed in more detail in Chapter 11.

While the Illinois GSA does not discriminate against single people embarking on a surrogacy arrangement, nor does it require the intended parents to be married, there are still certain requirements that potential intended parents must meet.[15]

| **Requirements for the Intended Parents[16]** |
|---|
| With respect to the intended parent or parents, the Act requires that:<br>1. At least one of the intended parents has contributed an egg or a sperm to create the "pre-embryo" that the surrogate will carry;<br>2. At least one has a certified medical need to proceed with surrogacy;<br>3. The intended parent or parents also complete a mental health evaluation; and<br>4. The intended parent or parents have consulted with an independent attorney regarding the surrogacy agreement. |

Under the Illinois GSA, at least one intended parent must donate a sperm or an egg to the formation of the embryo.[17] Further, the GSA does

14 *Id.*

15 *Id.* at § 20(b)(1)–(4).

16 *Id.*

17 *Id.* at § 20(b)(1).

require that any intended parent have a certified medical need for gestational surrogacy.[18]

Both of these requirements have been criticized as potentially being problematic and overly restrictive.[19] A single person with no fertility issues, for example, who wants to embark on surrogacy may not be able to get a doctor to certify their necessity, per the requirements of the statute (though technically a single person cannot create an embryo alone).[20] Since the definition of intended parent expressly includes single people, excluding a single person because they do not have medical issues with their own fertility does not seem to be in accord with the intent of the statute. A physician could easily certify such a person's need for surrogacy because they can't have a child alone. Nonetheless, this statutory requirement may present a challenge if a physician is unwilling to certify the need for surrogacy for the single person.[21]

Similarly, a couple who prefers surrogacy over adoption, but who are unable to donate sperm or eggs to the process might be precluded by the statute.[22] Normally, intended parents do contribute at least sperm or eggs. But if intended parents cannot do that, they still might want to proceed with surrogacy. They may want to use the sperm or eggs of related parties. They may simply want to proceed with

---

18 *Id.* at § 20(b)(2).

19 *See* Arshagouni, *supra* note 2, at 809–10.

20 *Id.*

21 *Id.*

22 *Id.* at 810.

surrogacy because they want more control over the birth of their child.

By contrast with these requirements in the Illinois GSA, the newer California surrogacy act does not require a physician to certify medical necessity of surrogacy, nor does it require that one of the intended parents be a gamete donor.[23] In fact, the California surrogacy act is quite permissive and focuses on courts enforcing the intent of the parties to a surrogacy agreement, so long as they are all represented by independent counsel.[24]

The last two of the requirements for intended parents under the Illinois GSA are identical to the requirements for the surrogate. The intended parents should complete a mental health consultation to make sure that they are mature and stable enough to go through with the surrogacy arrangement, and take custody of the child or children delivered. As shown above, a major risk of surrogacy is the surrogate attempting to keep custody of the child. It is also a great fear of many surrogates that the intended parent or parents will not take custody and thereby leave the child or children with the surrogate who likely does not want to have any more children of her own. Both fears are legitimate and well warranted.

Also, like the requirement for the surrogate, it is important that the intended parents have their own

[23] *Compare* CAL. FAM. CODE § 7962 (West 2023), *with* GSA, *supra* note 1.

[24] FAM. § 7962.

attorney to help them work through, negotiate, and understand the terms of their surrogacy agreement. This includes, among so many other issues, an understanding of what the intended parents are promising to pay the surrogate, whether and when the parties agree that a pregnancy may be terminated, and how the intended parents will establish parental rights and custody when the child is born. Thus, the intended parents should work with an attorney who can make sure that they understand and manage the risks involved with surrogacy.

The Illinois GSA has certain formal requirements for the surrogacy agreement. These requirements are reflected below.

| **Form Requirements for the Surrogacy Agreement**[25] |
| --- |
| The Act requires that the surrogacy agreement:<br>1. be in writing;<br>2. be executed before any medical procedures are done;<br>3. the surrogate and intended parent(s) must be represented by separate attorneys and sign acknowledgments that they understand their commitments;<br>4. any compensation to be paid must be put in an escrow account and disbursed by an escrow agent; and<br>5. be witnessed by two competent adults. |

[25] GSA, *supra* note 1, at § 25(b)(1)–(5).

The formal requirements for the surrogacy agreement are designed to make sure that the intentions of the parties to the surrogacy arrangement are clearly set forth and recorded in a written contract. The writing requirement for a contract is generally referred to as a statute of frauds. This requirement is designed to prevent fraud. A contract that is memorialized in writing gives objective evidence of the precise intentions of the parties. It also ensures that the parties review all of the terms and conditions contemplated. The requirement for two witnesses is designed to help safeguard against the production of any fraudulent agreement.

It is also important for all of the details of the arrangement to be worked out and agreed to (formally "executed") before any medical procedures take place. If the parties cannot come to a mutual agreement, then they should never begin medical procedures.

Once again, having separate attorneys representing each of the parties ensures that each party understands their commitments and is able to negotiate for the terms they want and need. This is one of the key safeguards against the exploitation of the surrogate, but also helps the intended parents structure the arrangement in the way that they want.

The requirement for an escrow account is designed to protect the surrogate against the intended parents not paying what they promise to pay in the surrogacy agreement. With this requirement, all the funds that are required to be paid under the agreement (and generally somewhat more) are deposited into a special bank account (the "escrow account"). Then the amounts are disbursed by a professional upon proof that certain milestone events have occurred. So, for example, a certain amount might be due to the surrogate when she undergoes an embryo transfer. Another amount might be due upon confirmation that the surrogate is three months pregnant. Then further amounts might be released to the surrogate after each month of her pregnancy, with a final disbursement upon a successful birth. Using an escrow account for the money that will ultimately be paid to the surrogate if there is a successful pregnancy, also assures the surrogate that there will be sufficient funds to compensate her for her services.

The Illinois GSA also requires the parties to include certain provisions in the surrogacy agreement. These provisions are below.

| **Contents of the Surrogacy Agreement**[26] |
| --- |
| The Act **requires** that the surrogacy agreement provide that:<br>1. the surrogate attempt to carry and give birth to one or more children for the intended parent(s);<br>2. the surrogate then give custody of the child to the intended parent(s); |

[26] *Id.* at § 25(c)–(d).

3. if the surrogate is married, her husband must also agree to give up custody of the child or children born to the intended parents; and
4. the intended parents agree to take custody and assume responsibility for any child born by the surrogate at birth.

The Act provides that the surrogacy agreement **may** include:

1. the surrogate's agreement to undergo any medical procedure or test deemed necessary or prudent for the health of the child or children she carries;
2. the surrogate's agreement to behave in ways the intended parents or relevant physicians believe is in the best interests of the health of the child or children she carries;
3. the intended parents' agreement to compensate the surrogate reasonably; and
4. the intended parents' agreement to reimburse the surrogate for reasonable expenses related to the surrogacy.

The required provisions for the agreement are at the heart of any surrogacy arrangement. Under the Illinois GSA, the surrogate and her spouse both must agree that she will work with the intended parents to get pregnant and deliver a healthy child or children.[27] The surrogate and her spouse both must also agree that the intended parents will be the legal

[27] *Id.* at § 25(c)(2)(i).

parents of the child or children born and that the surrogate and spouse will acknowledge that fact and act accordingly.[28] Lastly, the intended parents have to agree that they will acknowledge and honor the parenthood of the child and assume that role at the birth.[29]

The Illinois GSA also includes optional provisions. One important optional provision in the Illinois GSA is a requirement that the surrogate engage in or refrain from doing certain activities. These activities might include undergoing recommended medical tests or procedures. They also can include behavior commitments to live in a way that is beneficial to the health of the child or children that the surrogate will carry.[30] So, intended parents are likely to ask the surrogate to refrain from smoking, drinking alcohol, and using any illegal drugs during her pregnancy.

Recall from Chapter 3 that at least one legal scholar critical of surrogacy was concerned about the enforcement of behavioral restrictions on surrogates, like those permitted here by the Illinois GSA.[31] Her concern was that if courts allowed agreements limiting a surrogate's control over her own body, the surrogate's actual physical liberty would be

---

[28] *Id.* at § 25(c)(2)(ii).

[29] *Id.* at § 25(c)(4)(i)–(ii).

[30] *Id.* at § 25(d)(1)–(2).

[31] Sara L. Ainsworth, *Bearing Children, Bearing Risks: Feminist Leadership for Progressive Regulation of Compensated Surrogacy in the United States*, 89 WASH. L. REV. 1077, 1089–1091 (2014).

compromised.[32] In an extreme case, a surrogate may even agree to give control over medical decisions affecting her body to intended parents.[33]

But note that the Illinois GSA only permits such provisions and that they are subject to discussion and agreement with the surrogate with the advice and help of her attorney advocate. Assuming that there is no duress or undue influence involved, a surrogate, with the help of her attorney, should be able to craft any agreement on behavioral restrictions in a way that is acceptable to her.

The Illinois GSA provides express statutory authorization for the intended parents to compensate the surrogate.[34] The Illinois GSA allows not only reimbursement of the surrogate's expenses, but also "reasonable compensation" for her service.[35]

The key to the Illinois GSA is that if all of the requirements of the statute are met, then the intended parents are deemed to be the parents of the children born to the surrogate at the time of their birth.[36] Further, custody automatically vests in the intended parents immediately upon birth.[37] Thus, no court involvement is necessary to amend or restate any birth certificate.

---

[32] *Id.*

[33] *Id.*

[34] GSA, *supra* note 1, at § 25(d)(3).

[35] *Id.*

[36] *Id.* at § 15(b)(3).

[37] *Id.* at § 15(b)(5).

Even if there is not strict compliance with every requirement of the statute, the Illinois GSA instructs courts attempting to determine parental rights and custody to consider the intent of the parties set forth in the surrogacy agreement.[38] This focus on courts following the intent of the parties is reminiscent of the *Calvert* case out of California (discussed in Chapter 3). In that case, where the surrogate attempted to establish parental rights over the child born through surrogacy, the California court followed the intent of all of the parties in entering into the surrogacy arrangement and gave parental and custody rights to the intended parents.[39]

Other states have similar statutes governing surrogacy. The next chapter outlines the laws in each state. Review those provisions so that you can make an early assessment about whether the laws of your state will support you in your surrogacy journey, or whether you will want to consider proceeding under the laws a state that is supportive of surrogacy, like Illinois.

---

[38] *Id.* at § 25(e).

[39] Johnson v. Calvert, 851 P.2d 776, 782 (Cal. 1993).

# CHAPTER 6

# SURVEY OF STATE SURROGACY LAWS

One of the primary risks involved in any surrogacy arrangement is navigating the legal regulatory environment. Surrogacy laws differ in the United States on a state-by-state basis. This may seem odd to non-lawyers, as the rights and privileges of a citizen of the United States concerning surrogacy are now, at least partly, contingent on where that citizen lives. While there are many federal laws that are uniform throughout the states, many laws in the United States vary on a state-by-state basis as a result of the federalist system in the United States.

Marriage and family law is an area that has traditionally been left to each state to regulate as it deems fit.[1] Many scholars and jurists think that it is helpful to allow the law to develop separately in each state since it allows each state to be a laboratory for the next state considering regulation.[2] Any particular state can survey what other states have

---

[1] *See, e.g.*, Maynard v. Hill, 125 U.S. 190, 206 (1888); Loving v. Virginia, 388 U.S. 1, 7 (1967); *see also* Obergefell v. Hodges, 576 U.S. 644, 715 (2015) (Scalia, J., dissenting) (quoting U.S. v. Windsor, 570 U.S. 744, 767 (2013)) ("[T]he Federal Government, through our history, has deferred to state-law policy decisions with respect to domestic relations.").

[2] *E.g.*, New State Ice Co. v. Liebmann, 285 U.S. 262, 311 (1932) (Brandeis, L., dissenting) ("It is one of the happy incidents of the federal system that a single courageous state may, if its citizens choose, serve as a laboratory; and try novel social and economic experiments without risk to the rest of the country.").

done on a regulatory front, and then choose to adopt the laws that are appropriate for their own state.[3]

This chapter summarizes the current state of surrogacy law in each of the states in the United States. It is crucial for intended parents, as well as surrogates and others involved, to understand the surrogacy laws in their states.

But even if intended parents live in a state where commercial surrogacy agreements are not enforceable, they still have options. One option is to proceed by working with a surrogate who will physically be in a state where surrogacy agreements are enforceable during the pregnancy and birth.

Alternatively, intended parents might decide to proceed even in their home state where surrogacy is not allowed, but then explicitly choose to have their arrangement governed by the laws of a state that does support and enforce surrogacy arrangements.[4] Beware, though, this option is not without its own risks. Courts in the jurisdiction where the pregnancy and birth physically happen may need to determine the enforceability of that choice-of-law clause. There is a chance that such courts will deem choosing the law of a different state to be unenforceable as against the public policy of their state. Moreover, some state statutes, like Utah and Wyoming, as you will see, mandate that at least one of the intended parents be resident of that state for the statute to apply. These

---

3 *Id.*

4 *See* Hodas v. Morin, 814 N.E.2d 320, 324 (Mass. 2004).

alternatives are discussed in more detail in Chapter 4.

## 1. AN OVERVIEW OF THE SURROGACY LAWS

The laws relating to surrogacy in the United States often distinguish between surrogacy that is compensated, known as commercial surrogacy, and surrogacy that is not, often referred to as altruistic surrogacy.[5] In other words, there are states, like Louisiana, Nebraska, and Kentucky, that allow a woman to be a surrogate so long as she is not paid to do so or paid to give up custody of the child she will bear.[6] The idea is that someone paying a surrogate to carry or give up a child is offensive and similar to selling or renting the surrogate's body and then selling the resulting child. Indeed, someone may be willing to be an altruistic surrogate for free if she is a good friend or relative of an intended parent. Uncompensated surrogacy arrangements still generally allow the intended parent to pay for the surrogate's expenses in connection with the arrangement.[7]

---

5 *See, e.g.*, A.H.W. v. G.H.B., 772 A.2d 948, 953 (N.J. Super. Ct. Ch. Div. 2000) (indicating that surrogacy contracts in the absence of compensation are permitted, but surrogacy contracts for compensation are not).

6 *Id.* at 952.

7 VA. CODE ANN. § 20–156 (Westlaw 2023) (" 'Compensation' means payment . . . in excess of reasonable medical and ancillary costs."); VA. CODE ANN. § 20–162(A) (Westlaw 2023) ("[P]rovision . . . for compensation to be paid to the surrogate is void and unenforceable.").

Some advisors will recharacterize paid surrogacy arrangements as uncompensated arrangements by categorizing the pay as reimbursement for living expenses or foregone wages in order to qualify for statutory enforcement. That approach is risky since a court may recognize that the arrangement is indeed commercial surrogacy, and, therefore, refuse to enforce it.

The laws in this area are complicated and are subject to change as attitudes towards surrogacy evolve and more people turn to surrogacy as a way to start or expand their families. The discussion below only scratches the surface of the law in each state. If you decide to proceed under a particular state law, you should absolutely review the laws of that state with your attorney.

## 2. ALABAMA

Alabama law does not expressly either authorize or prohibit surrogacy agreements. Further, no cases in Alabama have directly addressed this issue. Consequently, it is unclear in Alabama whether a court would uphold and enforce a surrogacy arrangement.

Under the Alabama Adoption Code, it is a "Class C felony for any individual or agency to receive any money . . . for placing, assisting, or arranging for the placement of a minor for adoption."[8] However, the Alabama Code expressly excludes surrogate

[8] ALA. CODE § 26–10E–33(b) (Westlaw through 2023 1st Special Sess.) (effective Jan. 1, 2024).

motherhood from coverage under the section criminalizing child placement.[9]

A 1996 Alabama case involved parties to a surrogacy agreement, but did not specifically address the validity of the agreement.[10] In *Brasfield v. Brasfield*, the Court of Civil Appeals of Alabama upheld the trial court's award of custody to the intended mother in a surrogacy agreement.[11] In that case, the genetic father of the child and the intended mother were divorcing.[12] The genetic father contended the intended mother should not be awarded custody because she was not the natural mother of the child, who was born as a result of a surrogacy agreement.[13] The court awarded the intended mother custody based on the trial court's evaluation of the best interest of the child, but did not specifically address the enforceability of the surrogacy agreement.[14]

## 3. ALASKA

There is no legal authority in Alaska governing the enforceability of surrogacy agreements. The Alaska statutes are silent on the subject, and there are no instructive published Alaska opinions.

---

[9] *Id.* § 26–10E–33(c).

[10] Brasfield v. Brasfield, 679 So. 2d 1091 (Ala. Civ. App. 1996).

[11] *Id.* at 1095.

[12] *Id.* at 1092.

[13] *Id.*

[14] *Id.* at 1095.

## 4. ARIZONA

Arizona statutory law expressly prohibits surrogacy agreements.[15] In fact, the Arizona statute governing surrogacy provides that the surrogate is the legal mother of a child who is born as a result of a surrogacy contract.[16] If the surrogate is married, then her husband becomes the child's father.[17]

The law regarding surrogacy is, however, unclear in Arizona. In 1994, the Court of Appeals of Arizona found "that the surrogate statute affects a fundamental liberty interest."[18] The court also found that "[t]he surrogate statute as it exists violates the equal protection guarantees of the United States and Arizona Constitutions."[19] There are no published opinions reconciling the conflict between the Arizona surrogacy statute and the appellate court's decision.

## 5. ARKANSAS

Surrogacy agreements are expressly enforceable under Arkansas law.[20] The Arkansas statutes addressing surrogacy provide that the genetic father and intended mother are the parents of any child born as a result of a surrogacy agreement.[21]

---

15 ARIZ. REV. STAT. ANN. § 25–218(A) (West 2023).

16 *Id.* § 25–218(B).

17 *Id.* § 25–218(C).

18 Soos v. Superior Court, 897 P.2d 1356, 1361 (Ariz. Ct. App. 1994).

19 *Id.*

20 ARK. CODE ANN. § 9–10–201(b)–(c) (West 2023).

21 *Id.*

## 6. CALIFORNIA

California has a relatively long history of supporting surrogacy. California's surrogacy act went into effect in 2013. That statute specifically provides that surrogacy arrangements are permitted and enforceable, though they are subject to regulation.[22]

In a California case back in 1993, *Johnson v. Calvert*, the Supreme Court of California decided that a surrogacy agreement was enforceable in California.[23] In that case, the court wrote, "[a] woman who enters into a gestational surrogacy arrangement is not exercising her own right to make procreative choices; she is agreeing to provide a necessary and profoundly important service without (by definition) any expectation that she will raise the resulting child as her own."[24]

In 2005, the Supreme Court of California decided three companion cases to *Johnson v. Calvert* that involved lesbian couples who engaged in surrogacy agreements as a means of reproduction.[25] Those courts held that both people in a same-sex relationship can be the presumptive parents of a

---

[22] CAL. FAM. CODE § 7962 (West 2023).

[23] Johnson v. Calvert, 851 P.2d 776, 782 (Cal. 1993).

[24] *Id.* at 787.

[25] Elisa B. v. Superior Court, 117 P.3d 660 (Cal. 2005); Kristine H. v. Lisa R., 117 P.3d 690 (Cal. 2005); K.M. v. E.G., 117 P.3d 673 (Cal. 2005).

child born as a result of a surrogacy agreement even though one person is not the child's genetic parent.[26]

## 7. COLORADO

Surrogacy is specifically supported in Colorado pursuant to statute.[27] That statute, the Colorado Surrogacy Agreement Act, was just passed in 2021, and has a host of familiar requirements that must be met for a surrogacy agreement to be upheld.[28] Under this act, surrogates must be at least 21, have had a child previously, have mental health consultation and be represented by counsel.[29] Intended parents do not need to be married, straight, nor do they need to be genetically related to their child.[30]

## 8. CONNECTICUT

Surrogacy agreements are expressly legal and enforceable under Connecticut law.[31] Again, the statute has some basic requirements in order for the surrogacy agreement to be upheld. Surrogates need

---

[26] *See* Elise B., 117 P.3d. at 125 (concluding that even though one of the women was not the child's biological mother, she was still the presumptive parent because she "actively participated in causing the child[ ] to be conceived with the understanding that she would raise the child[ ] as her own together with the birth mother . . . .").

[27] COLO. REV. STAT. ANN. § 19–4.5–101 to –114 (West 2023).

[28] *Id.* § 19–4.5–104 (listing eligibility requirements; *Id.* § 19–4.5–105 (listing process requirements); *Id.* § 19–4.5–106 (listing surrogacy agreement requirements).

[29] *Id.* § 19–4.5–106(1).

[30] *See Id.* § 19–4.5–106(2).

[31] CONN. GEN. STAT. ANN. § 46b–532(a) (West 2023).

to be over 21, have a child previously, and all parties must have a mental health consultation and be represented by an attorney.[32]

## 9. DELAWARE

Surrogacy agreements are expressly legal and enforceable under Delaware law.[33] The Delaware Code provides that the purpose of the laws governing surrogacy is "to establish consistent standards and procedural safeguards for the protection of all parties to a gestational carrier agreement in [Delaware] . . . ."[34] Again, the statute has some basic requirements in order for the surrogacy agreement to be upheld. Surrogates need to be over 21, and have a child previously.[35] All parties should have a mental health consultation and be represented by an attorney.[36]

## 10. WASHINGTON D.C.

Surrogacy agreements are now expressly permitted in Washington D.C. in accord with the Collaborative Reproduction Amendment Act of 2016.[37] Like many surrogacy statutes, this statute has familiar requirements for the surrogate and for the intended parents. Surrogates need to be over 21,

---

[32] *Id.* § 46b–522.

[33] DEL. CODE ANN. tit. 13, § 8–807(a) (West 2023).

[34] *Id.* § 8–802(a).

[35] *Id.* § 8–806(a)(1)–(2).

[36] *Id.* § 8–806(a)(4)–(5), (b)(1)–(2).

[37] 64 D.C. Reg. 2037 (Feb. 24, 2017) (codified at D.C. CODE § 16–401 to –411 (2023)).

have a child previously, have a mental health consultation and be represented by an attorney.[38] Intended parents can be single or married. All parties also need to complete a mental health consultation and should be represented by an attorney.[39]

## 11. FLORIDA

Surrogacy agreements are expressly legal and enforceable under Florida law.[40] Florida, however, has the additional requirements that the intended parents must be married, and that "[t]he commissioning mother cannot physically gestate a pregnancy to term; [t]he gestation will cause a risk to the physical health of the commissioning mother; or [t]he gestation will cause a risk to the health of the fetus."[41] It is unclear how this health requirement could be met by two men in a same-sex marriage. Interestingly, Florida even allows women as young as 18 to be a surrogate, provided the rest of the statutory precautions are followed.[42]

## 12. GEORGIA

There is no legal authority in Georgia governing the enforceability of surrogacy agreements. The Georgia statutes are silent on the subject and there are no instructive published Georgia opinions.

---

38 D.C. CODE § 16–405(a) (2023).

39 *Id.* § 16–405(b).

40 FLA. STAT. ANN. § 742.15(1) (West 2023).

41 *Id.* § 742.15(2)(a)–(c).

42 *Id.* § 742.15(1).

## 13. HAWAII

There is no legal authority in Hawaii governing the enforceability of surrogacy agreements. The Hawaii statutes are silent on the subject and there are no instructive published Hawaii opinions.

## 14. IDAHO

The legislature of Idaho just passed a surrogacy statute that went into effect on July 1, 2023 that permits commercial gestational surrogacy in Idaho.[43] The new law, The Gestational Agreements Act, is subject to typical protections like all the parties being represented by counsel.[44] Traditional surrogacy arrangements, where the surrogate is genetically related to the child, are not allowed under this law.[45] The surrogacy agreement does have to be presented to the Idaho courts to verify conformity with the law.[46] But once approved, the surrogacy can proceed with the intended parent or parents getting parental rights upon the birth of their child or children.[47]

A 2016 opinion by the Supreme Court of Idaho indicated that surrogacy agreements were not likely to be enforceable in Idaho courts.[48] In that case the court held that the courts did not have the authority

---

[43] Idaho Code Ann. § 7–1604 (West).

[44] *Id.* § 7–1604(7).

[45] *Id.* § 7–1604(1) ("Neither the gestational carrier nor her spouse may contribute gametes for use in assisted reproduction under the gestational agreement.").

[46] *Id.* § 7–1605(1).

[47] *Id.* § 7–1605(4).

[48] *In re* Jane Doe, 372 P.3d 1106 (Idaho 2016).

to make a declaration as to the parental rights of the intended parents in a surrogacy agreement.[49] The lower court in that case had gone so far as to declare surrogacy agreements to be against the public policy of the state of Idaho.[50] The new statute reverses course for Idaho and brings Idaho into the growing list of states that permit and enforce commercial gestational surrogacy.

## 15. ILLINOIS

Surrogacy agreements are expressly legal and enforceable under Illinois statutory law.[51] The Illinois statute governing surrogacy agreements outlines a set of requirements for both the surrogate and the intended parents for the purpose of protecting all parties involved.[52] Like many statutes now, those requirements include the surrogate being over 21, and having had a child previously.[53] All parties must have a mental health consultation, and be represented by an attorney.[54] There is also the requirement that at least one of the intended parents contributes one of the gametes.[55] The Illinois statute is examined in some length in Chapter 5, as an early example of a statute that outlines best practices to protect all the parties involved.

---

49 *Id.* at 1108.

50 *Id.* at 1107.

51 750 ILL. COMP. STAT. ANN. 47 (West 2023).

52 *Id.* § 20.

53 *Id.* § 20(a)(1)–(2).

54 *Id.* § 20(a)(4)–(5), (b)(3)–(4).

55 *Id.* § 25(b)(1).

## 16. INDIANA

The Indiana Code expressly provides that surrogacy agreements are void, unenforceable, and against the public policy of the state of Indiana.[56] There is a current house bill that has been introduced in Indiana that would repeal this statute and adopt a statute to support and enforce surrogacy arrangements.[57]

## 17. IOWA

The Iowa Code does not speak specifically to the enforceability of surrogacy arrangements, but it does exclude surrogacy from laws forbidding purchase or sale of individuals.[58] Moreover, there is an Iowa administrative code section that describes how birth certificates should be issued in cases where there is a gestational surrogate.[59]

Most importantly, in 2018 the Iowa Supreme Court held that surrogacy agreements are enforceable and do not violate the public policy of Iowa.[60] As that court said, "[a] contrary holding

---

[56] IND. CODE ANN. § 31–20–1–1 (West 2023).

[57] H.B. 1267, 123rd Gen. Assemb., 1st Reg. Sess. (Ind. 2023).

[58] IOWA CODE ANN. § 710.11 (West 2023) ("A person commits a class 'C' felony when the person purchases or sells or attempts to purchase or sell an individual to another person. This section does not apply to a surrogate mother arrangement. For purposes of this section, a 'surrogate mother arrangement' means an arrangement whereby a female agrees to be artificially inseminated with the semen of a donor, to bear a child, and to relinquish all rights regarding that child to the donor or donor couple.").

[59] *Id.* § 641–99.15(2).

[60] P.M. v. T.B., 907 N.W.2d 522, 537 (Iowa 2018).

invalidating surrogacy contracts would deprive infertile couples of the opportunity to raise their own biological children and would limit the personal autonomy of women willing to serve as surrogates to carry and deliver a baby to be raised by other loving parents."[61]

## 18. KANSAS

There is no binding authority governing the enforceability of surrogacy agreements in Kansas. However, while dated, the Attorney General of Kansas has issued two opinions suggesting surrogacy agreements are against the public policy of Kansas.[62]

## 19. KENTUCKY

There is little binding authority governing the enforceability of surrogacy agreements specifically in Kentucky. However, there is a Kentucky statute that prohibits "a contract or agreement which would compensate a woman for her artificial insemination and subsequent termination of parental rights to a child born as a result of that artificial insemination."[63] While surrogacy involves an embryo transfer and not artificial insemination, this provision could be applied by analogy or extension to ban commercial surrogacy, or to indicate that any

---

[61] *Id.* at 525.

[62] KAN. ATT'Y GEN., OP. NO. 96-73, PAYMENT FOR ADOPTION (1996), https://ksag.washburnlaw.edu/opinions/1996/1996-073.htm; KAN. ATT'Y GEN., OP. NO. 82-150, Domestic Relations (1982), https://ksag.washburnlaw.edu/opinions/1982/1982-150.pdf.

[63] KY. REV. STAT. ANN. § 199.590(4) (West 2023).

payment for carrying a baby for another intended parent is contrary to the public policy of Kentucky.

While dated, a 1980 opinion from the Kentucky Attorney General did indicate that compensated surrogacy agreements are against the public policy of Kentucky.[64] A 1986 opinion from the Kentucky Supreme Court suggested that uncompensated surrogacy agreements are not void as against the public policy of Kentucky.[65] When read together, these authorities suggest that at least altruistic surrogacy agreements are enforceable and not void as against the public policy of Kentucky.

## 20. LOUISIANA

The Louisiana statute governing surrogacy provides that gestational surrogacy agreements are only enforceable if there is no compensation, and the intended parents are a married man and woman.[66] Further, the intended parents must contribute their own gametes.[67] There are other requirements too including judicial approval of the contract before an embryo transfer.[68] There can also be no provision

---

[64] KENTUCKY ATT'Y GEN., OP. NO. 2-588 (1981).

[65] Surrogate Parenting Assocs., Inc. v. Commonwealth, 704 S.W.2d 209, 214 (Ky. 1986) ("The surrogate parenting procedure as outlined in the [agreement between the surrogate and the intended parents] is not foreclosed by legislation now on the books.").

[66] LA. STAT. ANN. § 9:2720(C) (West 2023); *id.* § 9:2718.1(6).

[67] *Id.* § 9:2718.1(6).

[68] *Id.* § 9:2720(B).

requiring the surrogate to terminate the pregnancy under any circumstances.[69]

## 21. MAINE

Maine passed a surrogacy statute in 2016, providing that surrogacy agreements are enforceable, as long as the parties meet the requirements of the statute.[70] Some of the requirements are common among states where surrogacy is enforceable. The surrogate must be at least 21 and have had a child previously.[71] All the parties must have a mental health consultation before proceeding and each must be represented by counsel.[72] Also among those requirements in Maine is the requirement that at least one of the parties must be a legal resident of Maine.[73]

## 22. MARYLAND

Maryland statutory law does not speak directly on the enforceability of surrogacy agreements. However, a 2007 opinion from the Court of Appeals of Maryland clearly stated that compensated surrogacy agreements are illegal in Maryland.[74] The

---

69 *Id.* § 9:2720(D).

70 ME. REV. STAT. ANN. tit. 19-A §§ 1931–1939 (West 2023).

71 *Id.* § 1931(1)(A)–(B).

72 *Id.* § 1931(1)(C)–(D), (2)(A)–(B).

73 *Id.* § 1932(3)(C).

74 *In re* Roberto D.B., 923 A.2d 115, 130 (Md. 2007) ("It requires noting that surrogacy contracts, that is, payment of money for a child, are illegal in Maryland.").

enforceability of uncompensated surrogacy agreements is unclear.

## 23. MASSACHUSETTS

Massachusetts statutory law does not speak directly to the enforceability of surrogacy agreements. Opinions by the Massachusetts Supreme Judicial Court indicate that surrogacy agreements are enforceable in Massachusetts.

In 2001, the genetic parents in a surrogacy agreement sought a pre-birth order directing the hospital to enter the names of the intended parents as the parents of the unborn twin children.[75] The court granted injunctive relief and upheld the terms of the surrogacy agreement.[76] The court also called on the Massachusetts legislature to address questions related to the validity of surrogacy agreements. The court opined that the Massachusetts legislature needs to provide a "comprehensive set of laws that deal with the medical, legal, and ethical aspects of [surrogacy agreements]."[77]

In 2004, the court upheld the authority of a Massachusetts Probate and Family Court judge to issue a pre-birth judgment of parentage in an equity action brought by intended parents in a surrogacy

---

[75] Culliton v. Beth Israel Deaconess Med. Ctr., 756 N.E.2d 1133, 1135 (Mass. 2001).

[76] *Id.*

[77] *Id.* at 1139.

arrangement.[78] In that case, the court ordered the probate judge to enter a judgment "declaring the [intended parents] to be the legal parents of the unborn child . . . ."[79] The court ordered the hospital to "place the [intended parents'] names on the record of birth . . . listing the [intended parents] as the father and mother, respectively, of the child."[80]

## 24. MICHIGAN

Michigan statutory law governing enforceability of surrogacy agreements expressly provides that "[a] surrogate parentage contract is void and unenforceable as contrary to public policy."[81] That section defines "surrogate parentage contract" as "a contract, agreement, or arrangement in which a female agrees to conceive a child through natural or artificial insemination, or in which a female agrees to surrogate gestation, and to voluntarily relinquish her parental or custodial rights to the child."[82]

The statute makes surrogacy a misdemeanor for the parties to the arrangement and imposes a $10,000 fine or up to one year in prison or both.[83] The statute makes it a felony for third parties (like surrogacy agencies or attorneys) to assist in structuring the arrangement; and in that case

---

78 Hodas v. Morin, 814 N.E.2d 320, 321–22 (Mass. 2004).

79 *Id.* at 327.

80 *Id.*

81 MICH. COMP. LAWS ANN. § 722.855 (West 2023).

82 *Id.* § 722.853(i).

83 *Id.* § 722.859(2).

imposes a $50,000 fine or up to five years in prison or both.[84]

## 25. MINNESOTA

Minnesota does not have any statutes or any instructive published cases on surrogacy. But in *In re Baby Boy A.*, an unpublished appellate court opinion, a court does uphold a choice-of-law provision in a surrogacy agreement.[85]

In a somewhat more recent case, however, the state of Minnesota applied traditional parentage statutes to a traditional surrogacy arrangement and found the traditional surrogate to be the legal mother of the child born with two intended fathers.[86] One of the intended fathers was declared a legal parent as well, and custody ultimately was granted to the intended parents.[87] That court specifically declined to address the enforceability of the surrogacy arrangement itself.[88]

## 26. MISSISSIPPI

There is no legal authority in Mississippi governing the enforceability of surrogacy agreements. The Mississippi statutes are silent on

---

[84] *Id.* § 722.859(3).

[85] Baby Boy A. v. J.M.A., No. A07-452, 2007 WL 4304448, at *3 (Minn. Ct. App. Dec. 11, 2007). *See* discussion *supra* in Chapter 4.

[86] A.L.S. *ex rel* J.P. v. E.A.G., No. A10-443, 2010 WL 4181449, at *1 (Minn. Ct. App. Oct. 26, 2010).

[87] *Id.*

[88] *Id.* at *5.

the subject. And there are no instructive published Mississippi opinions.

## 27. MISSOURI

There is no statutory or case law controlling the enforceability of surrogacy agreements in Missouri. A paid surrogacy agreement could run afoul of Missouri criminal law. The Missouri law of trafficking in children makes it a Class D felony for any individual to give or receive compensation in exchange for termination of parental rights.[89] Thus, entering into a paid surrogacy agreement could result in a felony conviction for the intended parents and the surrogate.

## 28. MONTANA

There is no legal authority in Montana governing the enforceability of surrogacy agreements. The Montana statutes are silent on the subject and there are no instructive published Montana opinions.

## 29. NEBRASKA

Nebraska statute provides that "[a] surrogate parenthood contract entered into shall be void and unenforceable."[90] Further, the statute provides that "a surrogate parenthood contract shall mean a contract by which a woman is to be compensated for bearing a child of a man who is not her husband."[91]

---

[89] MO. ANN. REV. STAT. § 568.175 (West 2023).

[90] NEB. REV. STAT. § 25–21,200(1) (West 2023).

[91] *Id.* § 25–21,200(2).

The definition of a surrogate-parenthood contract indicates that paid surrogacy agreements are clearly unenforceable. Having said that, in 2023 there is currently proposed legislation in Nebraska that would repeal the prohibition on surrogacy.[92]

## 30. NEVADA

Under Nevada law, paid and unpaid surrogacy agreements are explicitly permitted and are enforceable in Nevada courts.[93] The Nevada statute includes the typical protection requiring each of the parties be represented by counsel.[94]

## 31. NEW HAMPSHIRE

Paid and unpaid surrogacy agreements are expressly enforceable under New Hampshire law.[95] The statute provides that "[a] gestational carrier agreement . . . is a legal contract that is presumed to be valid and enforceable and is legally enforceable by the court."[96] Again, the typical protections for the parties are required. The surrogate must be at least 21 and have had a baby previously.[97] All parties must have a mental health consultation and representation by an attorney.[98]

---

92 L.B. 89, 108th Legislature, 1st Sess. (Neb. 2023).

93 NEV. REV. STAT. ANN. § 126.710(3)–(4) (West 2023).

94 *Id.* § 126.750(2).

95 N.H. REV. STAT. ANN. § 168-B:11 (West 2023).

96 *Id.* § 168-B:10.

97 *Id.* § 168-B:9.

98 *Id.* § 168-B:8–9.

## 32. NEW JERSEY

The now-famous case *In re Baby M* from the late 1980s established that paid surrogacy agreements were not enforceable in New Jersey.[99] In 2018, New Jersey reversed course, and its legislature adopted a pro-surrogacy statute that does allow for the enforceability of gestational surrogacy arrangements.[100] Once again, typical protections are required. The surrogate must be at least 21 and have given birth previously.[101] All parties must have mental health evaluations, and be represented by an attorney.[102]

## 33. NEW MEXICO

New Mexico specifically passed statutory language that neither permits nor prohibits gestational surrogacy.[103] "The New Mexico Uniform Parentage Act does not authorize or prohibit an agreement between a woman and the intended parents," whereby a woman agrees to give birth for intended parents through assisted reproductive technology and relinquish all parental rights.[104] Accordingly, parties should be cautious if proceeding in New Mexico. As of 2023, however, there is proposed

---

[99] *In re* Baby M, 537 A.2d 1227, 1240 (N.J. 1988).

[100] N.J. STAT. ANN. § 9:17–65(c) (West 2023).

[101] *Id.* § 9:17–64(a).

[102] *Id.* § 9:17–64(a)–(b).

[103] N.M. STAT. ANN. § 40–11A–801 (2010).

[104] *Id.*

legislation that would allow for surrogacy arrangements in New Mexico.[105]

## 34. NEW YORK

Like many states, New York previously prohibited gestational surrogacy arrangements. Then, in 2020, New York adopted the Child Parent Security Act, a statute specifically allowing for and enforcing gestational surrogacy arrangements.[106] Once again, typical protections are required of all parties including mental health evaluations and representation by counsel.[107] New York also requires that at least one of the intended parents be a legal resident of New York.[108]

## 35. NORTH CAROLINA

North Carolina law does not speak directly to the enforceability of surrogacy agreements. The North Carolina General Statutes do, however, distinguish between lawful and unlawful payments related to adoption.[109] Lawful payments related to adoption include "[m]edical, hospital, nursing, pharmaceutical, traveling, or other similar expenses incurred by a mother or her child incident to the

---

[105] H.B. 305, 56th Legislature, 1st Sess. (N.M. 2023).

[106] N.Y. FAM. CT. LAW § 581–401 (McKinney 2023).

[107] *Id.* § 581–402.

[108] *Id.*

[109] *Compare* N.C. GEN. STAT. ANN. § 48–10–102(a) (West 2023) (outlining unlawful payments related to adoption under North Carolina law), *with* N.C. GEN. STAT. ANN. § 48–10–103(a) (West 2023) (outlining lawful payments related to adoption under North Carolina law).

pregnancy and birth or any illness of the adoptee."[110] Payments to a surrogate do not appear to be authorized.

## 36. NORTH DAKOTA

North Dakota law explicitly distinguishes traditional surrogacy from gestational surrogacy.[111] The North Dakota Status of Children of Assisted Conception Act states that "[a]ny agreement in which a woman agrees to become a surrogate or to relinquish that woman's rights and duties as a parent of a child conceived through assisted conception is void. The surrogate, however, is the mother of a resulting child . . . ."[112] "Surrogate" is defined as "an adult woman who enters into an agreement to bear a child conceived through assisted conception for intended parents."[113] Traditional surrogacy agreements, where the surrogate is biologically related to the child she carries, are therefore unenforceable.

The Act also provides, however, that "[a] child born to a gestational carrier is a child of the intended parents for all purposes and is not a child of the gestational carrier and the gestational carrier's

---

[110] § 48–10–103(a)(2).

[111] *Compare* N.D. CENT. CODE ANN. § 14–18–05 (West 2023) (establishing that traditional surrogacy agreements are void), *with* N.D. CENT CODE ANN. § 14-08-08 (West 2023) (establishing the enforceability of gestational carrier agreements).

[112] § 14–18–05.

[113] *Id.* § 14–18–01(3).

husband, if any."[114] "Gestational carrier" is defined as "an adult woman who enters into an agreement to have an embryo implanted in her and bear the resulting child for intended parents, where the embryo is conceived by using the egg and sperm of the intended parents."[115] Thus, gestational surrogacy agreements, where the intended parents are both the biological parents, are enforceable in North Dakota. This is fairly limiting as in many cases intended parents are using an egg donor.

## 37. OHIO

Ohio statutory law does not expressly address the enforceability of surrogacy agreements. Ohio case law, however, indicates that gestational surrogacy agreements are not prohibited by Ohio law and are therefore enforceable in an Ohio court.[116]

Ohio case law has also made clear that parental determinations in a gestational surrogacy situation should first take into account who the genetic parents are.[117] Unless those parties have waived parental rights, the law should give priority to those individuals as legal parents.[118] Thus, a gestational surrogate would not be able to contest the parental rights of any intended parents who are genetically

---

[114] *Id.* § 14–18–08.

[115] *Id.* § 14–18–01(2).

[116] S.N. v. M.B., 935 N.E.2d 463, 470–71 (Ohio Ct. App. 2010).

[117] Belsito v. Clark, 644 N.E.2d 760, 766 (Ct. Com. Pl. Ohio 1994).

[118] *Id.* at 767.

related to the child unless the intended parent has waived their parental rights.

## 38. OKLAHOMA

Oklahoma joined those states that allow for and enforce surrogacy arrangements in 2019 when it passed the Gestational Agreement Act.[119] Under that statute, gestational surrogacy is described as "important and selfless undertaking."[120] The act is designed to "ensure that gestational agreements will be enforced and that the expectations of the parties to gestational agreements will be protected."[121] Once again, typical protections for the parties are mandated. The surrogate must be over 21, have had a child before and have a mental health evaluation.[122] All parties must be represented by an independent attorney.[123]

## 39. OREGON

Oregon does not explicitly allow for the enforcement of surrogacy arrangements. Oregon statutory law, however, does indicate that surrogacy agreements are not against the public policy of Oregon. An Oregon statute provides that buying or selling a person who is less than 18 years of age is a Class B felony.[124] That section, however, explicitly

---

[119] OKLA. STAT. ANN. tit. 10, § 557 (West 2023).

[120] *Id.* § 10–557.1.

[121] *Id.*

[122] *Id.* § 10–557.4(A)(1)–(2), (5).

[123] *Id.* at § 10–557.6(A)(3).

[124] OR. REV. STAT. § 163.537(3) (West 2023).

does not "[a]pply to fees for services in an adoption pursuant to a surrogacy agreement."[125]

## 40. PENNSYLVANIA

Pennsylvania statutory law does not address the enforceability of surrogacy agreements. There is, however, caselaw in Pennsylvania indicating that surrogacy agreement will be upheld and enforced.

In 2006, the Superior Court of Pennsylvania overturned a lower court's decision granting custody of children born as a result of a surrogacy agreement to the gestational carrier.[126] That case involved a "biological father seeking custody of his children from a third party gestational carrier who [was] not the children's biological mother, and who took the children from the hospital in direct defiance of [the] [f]ather's wishes after she completely changed her mind about how matters would proceed."[127] The trial court voided the surrogacy contract and named the surrogate mother the child's legal mother, granting her standing.[128] The Superior Court rejected this reasoning—without any "biological connection to the child," the surrogate had no standing to seek custody.[129] The court, however, "declin[ed] to rule on the propriety of surrogacy contracts generally."[130] It

---

125 *Id.* § 163.537(2)(d).

126 J.F. v. D.B., 897 A.2d 1261, 1265 (Pa. Super. Ct. 2006).

127 *Id.* at 1280.

128 *Id.* at 1280.

129 *Id.*

130 *Id.*

reasoned that "[t]hat is a task for [Pennsylvania's] legislators."[131]

In 2015, an appellate court was faced with a surrogacy case where the intended parents had divorced and the ex-wife wanted to have their surrogacy agreement declared void in Pennsylvania as against public policy.[132] That court stated that "[a]bsent an established public policy to void the gestational carrier contract at issue, the contract remains binding and enforceable against Appellant."[133]

## 41. RHODE ISLAND

In 2021, Rhode Island also joined those states that allow for and enforce surrogacy arrangements when it amended its Uniform Parentage Act to include a section addressing surrogacy.[134] Those provisions also include the typical protections for the parties including mental health consultations and representations by attorneys in the process.[135]

## 42. SOUTH CAROLINA

There is no statutory authority in South Carolina governing the enforceability of surrogacy agreements. There is, however, a case from 2007 involving a dispute over insurance in a surrogacy

---

131 *Id.*

132 *In re* Baby S., 128 A.3d 296, 301 (Pa. Super. Ct. 2015).

133 *Id.* at 307.

134 15 R.I. GEN. LAWS ANN. § 15–8.1–801 to –809 (West 2023).

135 *Id.* at § 15–8.1–801; § 15–8.1–802.

situation where the South Carolina appellate court did look to the surrogacy agreement for insights into how to resolve this issue.[136]

The issue in that case was whether the child born to the surrogate could be considered the natural child of the husband of the surrogate.[137] If so, the insurance company would need to cover medical expenses related to the child. The court found that the surrogacy agreement referred to the child as the natural child of the intended parents and used that fact to buttress its holding for the insurance company.[138] In referring to and honoring the surrogacy agreement, the court implied that surrogacy agreements are valid and binding in South Carolina.

## 43. SOUTH DAKOTA

There is no legal authority in South Dakota governing the enforceability of surrogacy agreements. The South Dakota statutes are silent on the subject and there are no instructive published South Dakota opinions.

## 44. TENNESSEE

Surrogacy agreements are likely enforceable under Tennessee law. In 2014, the Supreme Court of Tennessee wrote that "the public policy of

---

136 Mid-South Ins. Co. v. Doe, 274 F.Supp.2d 757, 759–60 (D.S.C. 2003).

137 *Id.* at 761.

138 *Id.* at 762.

[Tennessee] does not preclude the enforcement of traditional surrogacy contracts. . . . the terms of a surrogacy contract may not circumvent the statutes governing a person's status as a legal parent or the statutory procedures for terminating parental rights."[139] The Tennessee Code also defines "surrogate birth" as:

> (i) The union of the wife's egg and the husband's sperm, which are then placed in another woman, who carries the fetus to term and who, pursuant to a contract, then relinquishes all parental rights to the child to the biological parents pursuant to the terms of the contract; or
>
> (ii) [t]he insemination of a woman by the sperm of a man under a contract by which the parties state their intent that the woman who carries the fetus shall relinquish the child to the biological father and the biological father's wife to parent.[140]

The Tennessee Code also provides for a streamlined process for intended parents to establish their parental rights. Where there is an embryo transfer the intended parents need not go through the adoptive process to establish parentage in Tennessee.[141]

---

[139] *In re* Baby, 447 S.W.3d 807, 833 (Tenn. 2014).

[140] TENN. CODE ANN. § 36–1–102(52)(A)(i)–(ii) (West 2023).

[141] *Id.* § 36–2–401.

When read all together, the case and statutory provisions seem to indicate that surrogacy arrangements, wherein the intended parents are both the genetic parents of the child, are enforceable. Furthermore, surrogacy arrangements, wherein the surrogate is the genetic mother and the intended father is the genetic father, are also enforceable. It is unclear, however, whether a Tennessee court would enforce a surrogacy agreement where there is a third-party egg donor. The statute specifically states that nothing in it should be construed as authorizing the surrogate birth process.[142]

## 45. TEXAS

Gestational surrogacy agreements are expressly enforceable under Texas law.[143] The Texas Family Code also expressly requires that "[t]he intended parents must be married to each other" and that "[e]ach intended parent must be a party to the gestational agreement."[144] So a surrogacy arrangement with a single intended parent appears not to be allowed in Texas.

Also the agreement must be validated by a court in its discretion.[145] Further, either the surrogate or the intended parents must have resided in Texas for at

---

142 *Id.* § 36–1–102(52)(C).

143 TEX. FAM. CODE ANN. § 160.752(a) (West 2023).

144 *Id.* § 160.754(b).

145 *Id.* § 160.755.

least 90 days prior petitioning the court to validate the agreement.[146]

## 46. UTAH

The Utah statute governing the enforceability of surrogacy agreements expressly provides that compensated and uncompensated surrogacy agreements are enforceable if they conform to strict requirements.[147] The Utah statute is similar to the Texas statute in that the intended parents must be married.[148] So, again, it appears that single intended parents are excluded. Further, again as in Texas, the surrogacy agreement has to be approved by the court and either the surrogate or the intended parents have to have been residents of Utah for at least 90 days before the petition is made.[149]

In 2019, the Supreme Court of Utah affirmed that the Utah surrogacy statute also allows same-sex male couples who are married to enforce surrogacy agreements.[150] That court reasoned that the opposite result (arrived at by the district court) violated the United States Constitution.[151]

---

146 *Id.*

147 UTAH CODE ANN. § 78B–15–801(4) (West 2023).

148 *Id.* § 78B–15–801(3).

149 *Id.* § 78B–15–802(1)–(2).

150 *In re* Gestational Agreement, 2019 UT 40, 449 P.3d 69.

151 *Id.* at 73.

## 47. VERMONT

Vermont passed a Parentage by Gestational Carrier Agreement statute in 2017.[152] Under the Vermont statute, surrogacy agreements are valid and enforceable subject to the requirements of the statute. Among those requirements are mental health consultations and independent legal representation for all the parties.[153]

## 48. VIRGINIA

Surrogacy is allowed in Virginia but there can be no compensation beyond medical and other ancillary expenses. "All the parties . . . understand that any agreement between them for payment of compensation is void and unenforceable."[154] This, in fact, excludes typical surrogacy arrangements where the surrogate is being compensated for her services.

Nonetheless, the Virginia statute governing the enforceability of surrogacy agreements expressly provides that "[a] surrogate, her spouse, if any, and the prospective intended parent may enter into a written agreement whereby the surrogate may relinquish all her rights and duties as parent of a child conceived through assisted conception, and the prospective intended parent may become the parent of the child . . . ."[155]

---

[152] VT. STAT. ANN. tit. 15C §§ 801–809 (West 2023).

[153] *Id.* § 801(a)(2)–(3).

[154] VA. CODE ANN. § 20–160(B)(4) (West 2023).

[155] *Id.* § 20–159(A).

## 49. WASHINGTON

Washington amended its Uniform Parentage Act in 2018 to allow for and enforce surrogacy arrangements.[156] Like many states, Washington has a host of requirements to protect the parties. The surrogate must be at least 21 and have given birth previously.[157] All parties must submit to a mental health consultation and each of the parties must have independent counsel.[158]

## 50. WEST VIRGINIA

The law governing surrogacy agreements in West Virginia is unclear. The Code of West Virginia does not speak directly to the enforceability of surrogacy agreements. The Code does, however, exclude surrogacy from laws that prohibit the purchase or sale of a child.[159]

## 51. WISCONSIN

Wisconsin statutory law does not directly speak to the enforceability of surrogacy contracts. In 2013, however, the Supreme Court of Wisconsin held that surrogacy agreements are enforceable. The court reasoned that enforcing surrogacy agreements "promotes stability and permanence in family

---

156 WASH. REV. CODE ANN. § 26.26A.700–785 (West 2023).

157 *Id.* § 26.26A.705(1)(a)–(b).

158 *Id.* § 26.26A.705(1)(d)–(e), (2)(c)–(d).

159 W. VA. CODE § 61–2–14h(e)(3) (West 20123) ("This section [on trafficking in children] does not prohibit . . . [f]ees and expenses included in any agreement in which a woman agrees to become a surrogate mother.").

relationships because it allows the intended parents to plan for the arrival of their child, reinforces the expectations of all parties of the agreement, and reduces contentious litigation that could drag on for the first several years of the child's life."[160]

That court also held that surrogacy agreements are not void as against the public policy of Wisconsin.[161] The court determined that surrogacy agreements are "enforceable contract[s] unless enforcement is contrary to the best interest of [the child]."[162] Finally, the court "respectfully urge[d] the [Wisconsin] legislature to consider enacting legislation regarding surrogacy."[163]

## 52. WYOMING

Wyoming does have statutory authority regarding surrogacy arrangements, but like Virginia, mandates that there be no compensation beyond medical expenses and other amounts incidental to the pregnancy.[164] This excludes most typical surrogacy arrangements where the surrogate is in fact compensated for her services. Beyond that requirement, there must be two intended parents[165] and both must have been citizens of Wyoming for at

---

160 *In re* F.T.R., 833 N.W.2d 634, 652 (Wis. 2013).

161 *Id.*

162 *Id.*

163 *Id.* at 653.

164 WYO. STAT. ANN. § 35–1–401(a)(xiv)(G) (West 2023).

165 *Id.* § 35–1–401(a)(xvi).

least a year preceding the date of the surrogacy agreement.[166]

[166] *Id.* § 35–1–401(a)(xiv)(E) (2021).

# CHAPTER 7
# THE SURROGACY AGREEMENT

A contract is simply a set of promises between parties that is legally binding.[1] Thus, not surprisingly, a surrogacy agreement is a contract. The structure for any surrogacy arrangement is set forth in the agreement between the parties. The surrogacy agreement is a roadmap for how the relationship between the intended parents and the surrogate will proceed. Thinking through that agreement, drafting it, negotiating it, and executing it helps the parties further contemplate and understand the scope of their rights and obligations and the gravity of the arrangement.

But note that breaking a contract does not mean that the breaching party has broken the law. It merely means that the other party or parties may have remedies available to them for the breach and that those remedies might be enforced by a court of law. This is important to understand.

So, for example, if a surrogate aborts a child being carried for an intended parent against the intended parent's wishes and in contravention of the parties' agreement, any remedy granted to the intended parent may seem insufficient. Indeed, what remedy might a court impose? Any large monetary damages

---

[1] Section 1 of the Restatement (Second) of Contracts defines a contract as "a promise or a set of promises for the breach of which the law gives a remedy, or the performance of which the law in some way recognizes as a duty." RESTATEMENT (SECOND) OF CONTRACTS § 1 (AM. L. INST. 1981).

might be unrecoverable if the surrogate simply can't pay those penalties. And money as a remedy for that kind of breach seems insufficient in any event. Understanding that some of the most vital parts of the surrogacy arrangement cannot be fully policed or enforced by the law underscores the fact that there are inherent risks in the arrangement. Working through the contract and the expectations should help make sure that the parties understand the gravity of the arrangement and will abide by their agreement. But there is always risk.

As reflected in the Illinois Gestational Surrogacy Act (the Illinois GSA) discussed in Chapter 5, there are certain provisions that are fundamental in any surrogacy contract. These provisions include the surrogate's agreement to attempt to become pregnant and the agreement that parental rights and custody of any resulting children vests with the intended parent or parents. The Illinois GSA legally requires that those central provisions be present in the agreement.[2]

Beyond those few required provisions, however, there are many issues that the parties should consider and agree upon prior to executing a surrogacy arrangement. This chapter will consider the types of provisions that should be included and will highlight the interests at stake for the intended parents and the surrogate. Again, please note that often I use intended parents in the plural for

---

[2] 750 ILL. COMP. STAT. 47/25(c)(1) (West 2023).

convenience sake, but that all of these issues apply to a single intended parent as well.

## 1. USE YOUR ATTORNEY AND UNDERSTAND YOUR CONTRACT

Both the intended parents and the surrogate should be represented by independent attorneys when preparing and negotiating the surrogacy agreement. This is required by the Illinois GSA and reflects best practices around the country. Attorneys help each of the parties fully understand the implications of their agreement and the range of alternatives available. Typically, all of the attorney fees are paid by the intended parent or parents as another cost associated with surrogacy.

As mentioned, one of the functions of the contracting process is to make sure the parties understand what they are committing to do. Parties sometimes rely too heavily on their attorneys and do not always read through the entire contract.

I always joke with my law students who are studying contract law that the first three rules crucial to understanding a contract are:

(i) read the contract,

(ii) read the contract, and

(iii) read the $#%-ing contract.

While it may not be easy reading, it is crucial, especially in an important and complex arrangement like surrogacy, for each of the parties to read through the contract thoroughly and understand their commitments, or negotiate for different terms.

There are general tensions and principles that exist with drafting contracts. First, there is a general tendency for attorneys to write agreements using overly complex sentences and language. Best practices dictate that contracts should be written in plain English. This means that contract drafters should write every sentence in plain English so that the agreement is easy to read.

**Understanding Your Contract**

If you don't understand any provision written into your contract, ask your lawyer to re-write the provision so that it is clear. Never agree to anything you don't understand.

Another tension that exists in contract drafting is the tension between being brief and including too much detail. A brief contract is less inclusive, but it may be easier for a reader to understand. A detailed contract is more thorough, but it may be more difficult for the reader to understand. There is a middle ground that provides a balance between brief and detailed contracts. Every attorney has his or her own approach to striking this balance.

Intended parents and surrogates should work with their own attorney to develop a surrogacy agreement that works for their unique set of circumstances. This chapter provides sample language to illustrate what a basic surrogacy contract may look like. The sample provisions provide guidance on the issues involved and how the parties may address them in their own agreement.

## A. PREFATORY CLAUSES

Contracts typically begin with a set of prefatory paragraphs that explain the setting for the arrangement that is the subject of the agreement and set the tone for the entire agreement. Each prefatory paragraph may be identified by a sequential number or letter; or the clauses may each begin with the word "Whereas."

In practice, the prefatory clauses usually do not contain the promises that a court would need to enforce. However, prefatory clauses provide useful background information that a court may use to establish the intent of the parties. Sample prefatory clauses are shown below.

| **Prefatory Clauses** |
|---|
| **Whereas:** the Intended Parents are unable to have natural children of their own, and seek to work with a surrogate to have one or more biologically related children; and |
| **Whereas:** the Surrogate is sympathetic to the needs of the intended parents, and seeks to help the intended parents have one or more children by embarking on the surrogacy arrangement described herein; and |
| **Whereas:** as a result, the Intended Parents are incredibly appreciative of Surrogate's willingness |

to help and commit to compensate her as outlined in this agreement; and

**Whereas:** the parties understand that all the medical procedures associated with this surrogacy arrangement, including pregnancy and childbirth, are inherently risky; and

**Whereas:** notwithstanding those risks, the parties to this agreement herein set forth with specificity their mutual intention that the Surrogate: (i) be impregnated with one or more embryos created with the sperm of the Intended Father and the egg of an Egg Donor, and (ii) ultimately birth one or more children for the Intended Parents; and

**Whereas:** the Intended Parents will take full parental responsibility for, and custody of, the children so born; and neither the surrogate nor her spouse will have any legal relationship with the children so born;

Now therefore, the parties agree . . . .

These major issues will also be set forth in greater detail further into the agreement. Thus, how much detail and how much discussion to put into the prefatory clauses is a question of balance. Drafters should highlight important details up front to be sure that the intent of the parties is fully clear. However, the detail of the arrangement can be left for the later sections.

The prefatory provisions are also a good place for language that can help build a positive relationship between the parties. In the sample clauses above, a provision was added to compliment the surrogate for being sympathetic towards the intended parents. Instead of focusing on the dangers of surrogacy, the clause applauds the surrogate for her generous service.

The sample clause that begins with "Whereas, the Intended Parents are incredibly appreciative of Surrogate's willingness to help. . ." reflects the intended parents' gratitude towards the surrogate. Parties may also want to mention a specific situation that brought the particular intended parents and surrogate together. The prefatory clauses set the theme and tone for the surrogacy relationship, so infusing them with positivity helps the parties achieve a successful cooperative relationship and feel good in the process.

**Tales from the Field: Beware Being Overly Aggressive**

In our first surrogacy agreement, the drafting attorney working for the us as the intended parents decided to emphasize in the prefatory clauses the high degree of risk that the surrogate was undertaking to be sure she understood that risk. The agreement therefore included language about the parties understanding that pregnancy carries with it a high degree of risk, even risk of death and that the parties still willingly agreed to undertake the arrangement.

The language used in that contract went on to explain that if the surrogate were to suffer from

> some medical condition during the pregnancy such that she could not make her own medical decisions, then the intended parents would be authorized to make decisions for her since the life and health of their children were involved.
>
> And that contract further stated that even if the surrogate were to be in a vegetative coma, the intended parents would be authorized to make those medical decisions that would sustain the vegetative body of the surrogate sufficiently to allow for the children to be born as healthy as possible.
>
> All of these provisions protected the intended parents and were good for the surrogate to consider before moving forward. However, the extreme nature of the language, including the specter of the surrogate dropping dead or falling into a vegetative coma as a result of the pregnancy, were enough to just about scare our surrogate off all together.
>
> Thus, when drafting and including language, parties should be sensitive to the purpose of the language. It is appropriate for attorneys to apprise parties of the risk and make provisions for what will happen in certain unplanned, even unfortunate, circumstances. Language that is overly aggressive, however, may only serve to destroy an otherwise potentially cooperative relationship.

Note from the example above, that the contract language contemplated the Intended Parents being able to make medical decisions for the surrogate if she were unable to make those decisions for herself. This is just the kind of aggressive arrangement that critics of surrogacy have found objectionable.[3] This kind of agreement cedes control over the surrogate's medical decisions to the intended parents and divests the surrogate of control over her own body.

Of course, individuals do have the right to authorize others to make medical decisions for them when they are incapacitated. That is routinely done with health care power of attorney agreements. However, it is not routinely the case that someone cedes health care decisions, even involving life or death, to a third party who is paying them to perform a service. It is unclear whether such a provision would even be legally binding if challenged. This kind of provision may well be found to be unenforceable as against public policy or even unconscionable.

A better approach might well be a collaborative and respectful approach that commits all the parties to cooperate and consider the life of the fetus in the case of a crisis when the surrogate can no longer make her own healthcare decisions. Respect and cooperation are the hallmarks of any successful relationship between a surrogate and her intended parent(s).

---

[3] Sara L. Ainsworth, *Bearing Children, Bearing Risks: Feminist Leadership for Progressive Regulation of Compensated Surrogacy in the United States*, 89 WASH. L. REV. 1077, 1089 (2014).

**Sample Provision Re: Incapacity**

**Whereas:** the parties recognize that unfortunate circumstances may arise when the Surrogate becomes incapacitated and cannot make healthcare decisions for herself; in such a case, the surrogate's [partner, spouse or parents] will consult with the intended parents and use best efforts to make healthcare decisions for the Surrogate that protect and preserve the life of any fetus being carried by the Surrogate.

## B. DEFINITIONS

Capitalized words are generally words that have specific definitions assigned to them somewhere in the agreement. In simple agreements, drafters may set forth the definition when they first use a term. Drafters also generally put the term in capital letters and parenthesis to show that it is a defined term. In longer and more complex agreements, there is usually a section dedicated to definitions. That section is likely to be at the beginning of the agreement so that it is easy for the reader to find and understand the terms before reading the contract.

Casual readers of contracts tend to skim over the definition section. Parties should beware not to do this. Sometimes definitions may change the rights or obligations of the parties. For example, the definitions may set forth when an abortion is permissible as shown below.

| Definitions |
| --- |
| **Permitted Abortion**—an abortion in the first twenty weeks of pregnancy (measured from the date of insemination) requested by the Intended Parents or certified to be medically necessary by a Responsible Physician for the life or health of the Surrogate or the Child. |

Later in the agreement, the relevant section may only say, "the Surrogate agrees not to have an abortion other than a Permitted Abortion." Thus, the crux of the agreement on when an abortion is permitted is actually in the definition. In this example, an abortion is essentially not a choice for the surrogate, but is one that is up to the discretion of the intended parents, unless it is medically required as certified by a responsible physician.

Substantively, this kind of provision again involves a situation where the Surrogate is agreeing to give control over medical decisions affecting her body to the intended parents. As indicated above, agreements that give third parties control over a person's healthcare decisions may not even be legally enforceable. They may be found to be against public policy or even unconscionable. Nonetheless, surrogates may want to consider carefully whether they are comfortable with that kind of agreement, and may well want to limit the ability of any intended parent to demand an abortion.

This particular definition of "Permitted Abortion" also sets forth the time frame when an abortion can be requested, in this case, within the first twenty weeks of pregnancy. That time frame may be controversial as well since a surrogate may not want to have an abortion after a shorter period of time, for example, twelve weeks. The definition also determines the date that timeline begins. In this example, that start date is the date of insemination. Some professionals may start counting the twenty weeks at the end of the last menstrual cycle. Thus, the twenty-week period defined by this agreement may actually represent more than twenty weeks to others who would start calculating the time at a different point.

The example definition of *Permitted Abortion* contains several other defined terms. These terms include *Intended Parents*, *Responsible Physician*, *Surrogate*, and *Child*. To fully understand the primary term, the reader must understand all of the other terms used within the definition.

A contractual definition of a term may not be the definition you would normally associate with the term. A term can have additional meanings other than its common usage. This warrants caution when drafting surrogacy contracts.

For example, without a specific definition, *Intended Parents* commonly means the person or couple seeking to have a child with the surrogate. However, a definition within a contract may also include how to proceed if the *Intended Parents* begin the process as a couple, but then end up separating before the process is complete. In this situation, if the intended parents are a married man and woman who used the husband's sperm to fertilize a donor egg, then the couple may decide in advance that if they divorce, *Intended Parents* might refer only to the husband.

*Surrogate* as a term should be straightforward as there is only ever one surrogate. Still, the definition of *Surrogate* may include a statement that it is "the woman who agrees to act as a surrogate under the terms of the agreement, unless she becomes pregnant with a child genetically unrelated to the *Intended Parents*, in which case any rights or privileges she may have had under the agreement do not apply to her." If the intended surrogate actually does get pregnant with a child not genetically related to the *Intended Parents*, then she would presumably no longer be deemed to be the *Surrogate*, as defined in the agreement.

*Responsible Physician* is a term often used by drafters. The drafter may define *Responsible Physician* as "the obstetrician who will be primarily responsible for the pregnancy and who is consented to by the Intended Parents and the Surrogate, or any subsequent obstetrician whose service is consented to by the Intended Parents and the Surrogate." Alternatively, the drafter may define the term more broadly to be "any physician coordinating, supervising, and attending to any of the procedures involved in getting the surrogate pregnant and monitoring that pregnancy through to childbirth."

The definition for the term *Child* could also be different than the plain meaning of the word. The term may be defined to mean "any fetus carried by the Surrogate and any child born as a result of the surrogacy process, but only where that child is genetically linked to the Intended Parents." This definition may be used later in the agreement to say, for example, that the *Intended Parents* will take full parental responsibility over any *Child* born through the surrogacy process. That statement allows the *Intended Parents* to avoid taking responsibility for any child that is not genetically linked to them. As a result, if the surrogate was in fact impregnated by her husband or any other man, then the *Intended Parents* would not be responsible for the resulting child.

Definitions can be crucial to establishing the rights and obligations of the parties and should not be ignored by drafters or readers. A full understanding of all of the rights and responsibilities of each party is more likely to result in full compliance with those rights and responsibilities after the agreement is executed. Drafters and parties to the agreement should never let a definition escape their notice.

## C. REPRESENTATIONS

In most sophisticated contracts there is a section where the parties attest to the truth of a series of representations. The representations are statements of fact that are relevant to the arrangement being contemplated. The other party relies on these statements when entering the agreement. If any representation turns out to be false, then the counterparty may have a legal basis on which to avoid any of his or her obligations under the agreement.

### 1) Representations of the Surrogate

The intended parents will likely want the surrogate to attest to a variety of facts, some of which may be required by law. For example, the Illinois GSA requires that the surrogate be over twenty-one, have had at least one child before becoming a surrogate, and have received both mental health and legal counseling. Thus, the party drafting the first version of the agreement will include a variety of standard representations that it wants the other party to make, and certain ones that it is willing to make. The parties then review the first version to make sure that all of the representations set forth are actually true. Any misstatement in this section could alleviate the intended parents of their obligations, since those obligations are considered contingent on the representations being true.

**Representations of the Surrogate**

The intended parents will want the surrogate to attest to a variety of facts. Some of these may include:

- that she is of a certain age (over 21 in any event);
- that she is either single or married (if married, the spouse will generally be required to sign on to the agreement);

- that she is competent to execute the agreement and fully understands the nature of the surrogacy arrangement;
- she is healthy and, at least to the best of her knowledge, can carry a child through pregnancy to birth;
- that she has had one or more children of her own previously;
- whether she has had any miscarriages or other problems with carrying a child to full term and birthing that child;
- that she fully understands the risks, both medical and psychological, associated with being a surrogate, becoming pregnant and carrying and birthing a child, including, in the extreme, complications from the pregnancy that could even lead to her own death;
- that she has received mental health counseling about the obligations and risks associated with surrogacy; and
- that she has received legal counseling about her risks, rights, and obligations as they pertain to surrogacy generally, and also as they are described in the surrogacy agreement.

Working through the draft agreement and asking the parties to attest to these statements will spark conversations between the parties where there are complicated facts or inaccuracies. For example, there may have been some medical issues that the surrogate had when trying to become pregnant or give birth in the past. The intended parents will want to know about those issues. Having those conversations in the course of the negotiations is crucial to the parties' ability to understand each other before proceeding with the arrangement.

### 2) Representations of the Intended Parents

As much as the intended parents want certain representations from the surrogate, the surrogate will want the intended parents to make certain representations as well. Some of these representations may also be required by the relevant law. For example, the Illinois GSA also requires intended parents to receive mental health and legal counseling before entering into the arrangement.

If, as is often the case, the intended parents provide the initial draft of the agreement, then the surrogate and her attorney may well ask for additional representations to be made by the intended parents beyond those already included in that first draft. The surrogate enters into the arrangement at least in part based on the truth of these representations. Thus, if any were untrue, then legally her obligations under the agreement may also be avoided. Below are sample representations of the intended parents.

**Representations of the Intended Parents**

The surrogate will want the intended parents to attest to a variety of facts. Some of these may include:

- that the intended parent(s) is either a single person or that they are part of a couple, married or otherwise (if part of a couple, the partner or spouse will generally be required to sign on to the agreement);
- that they are competent to execute the agreement and fully understand the nature of the surrogacy arrangement;
- that surrogacy has been certified as medically necessary for the intended parent(s);
- that at least one of the intended parents will contribute their own genetic material to create the embryo or embryos that will be used in the surrogacy arrangement;
- that they are healthy and, at least to the best of their knowledge, the contribution of their genetic material to the surrogate will not create any health risk for the surrogate;
- that they are healthy and, at least to the best of their knowledge, will be able to raise any children born from the surrogacy through to adulthood;
- that if anything should happen to them, including death, and they were not capable of raising any child born as a result of the

surrogacy, that they have appointed another named person to be the custodian of such child or children and that person has agreed;

- that they fully understand the risks, both medical and psychological, associated with surrogacy, including the fact that IVF is not always successful, nor does every pregnancy result in a live birth, due to no fault of the surrogate;
- that they have received mental health counseling about the obligations and risks associated with surrogacy;
- that they have received legal counseling about their risks, rights, and obligations as they pertain to surrogacy generally, and also as they are described in the surrogacy agreement;
- that they are financially capable of funding their obligations hereunder, have set up an escrow for payments for the surrogate, and understand that overall costs may end up surpassing any initial estimates; and
- that the intended parents have purchases appropriate medical insurance for the surrogate to cover her pregnancy and at least eight weeks after the birth of any children born from the surrogacy arrangement.

## D. MEDICAL TESTING AND AGREEMENT TO SHARE INFORMATION

After the definitions and representations, the next part of the contract addresses the early stages of what actually happens in a surrogacy arrangement. This section discusses the rights and obligations of the parties with respect to preliminary medical testing.

### 1) Medical Testing of the Surrogate

In any surrogacy arrangement, one of the first medical steps is the medical and mental health examinations of the surrogate and the intended parents to ensure that they are fit for their roles. The intended parents will want certain assurances about the surrogate and the surrogate will want certain assurances about the intended parents.

The intended parents will want to know, to the fullest extent possible, that the surrogate is medically fit to respond to the prescribed medications, become pregnant, and carry one or more child through to a live birth. In addition, the intended parents will want to be sure that the surrogate is not using narcotics or other drugs that may affect the health of any embryo or fetus. Further, the intended parents will want to know that the surrogate does not have any diseases or infections that could be transmitted to a child carried by her.

Accordingly, the surrogate will likely agree in this section to submit to all relevant medical examinations and tests designed to give the intended parents the assurances they need.

| Testing of Surrogate |
| --- |
| **Surrogate's Agreement to Submit to Testing.** The Surrogate agrees to submit to any and all medical and drug testing deemed prudent or required by any Responsible Physician. |

### 2) Medical Testing of the Intended Parents

As with any contract, there should be parallel rights and responsibilities of all the parties where applicable. In a surrogacy contract, the surrogate will likely want to make sure that the intended parents are healthy and able to raise the children to adulthood. The surrogate will also likely want to make sure that whoever is contributing genetic material to the embryo implanted in her will not be putting her health at risk. As a result, the contract should include a clause similar to the clause set forth above where the intended parents agree to any and all relevant medical tests.

| Testing of Intended Parents |
| --- |
| **Intended Parents' Agreement to Submit to Testing.** The Intended Parents agree to submit to any and all medical and drug testing deemed prudent or required by any Responsible Physician. |

### 3) Mental Health Counseling for All Parties

Certain state statutes (including the Illinois GSA) require mental health evaluations of the surrogate and the intended parents. The contract needs to have a section where the parties agree to submit to this testing. Any previous medical testing clauses may also contain reference to mental health evaluations or one clause may be used to capture all of these commitments.

| Testing on All Parties |
| --- |
| **The Parties' Agreement to Submit to Testing.** The Surrogate and the Intended Parents agree to submit to any and all medical tests that any Responsible Physician deems prudent or required. In addition, the Surrogate and the Intended Parents agree to submit to a mental health evaluation session with a counselor recommended or approved by any Responsible Physician. |

### 4) Agreement to Share Information

Related to the medical and psychological exams that the parties will undergo is the need for each of the parties to have access to the test results of the other party. An additional commitment to share information is generally required from all parties.

| Sharing Information |
| --- |
| **Agreement to Share Information.** The Surrogate and the Intended Parents agree to provide each other and all Responsible Physicians |

with access to the results of all relevant medical and psychological tests and to execute any additional documents necessary to assure that access.

### 5) Termination if Testing Is Unsatisfactory

There needs to be a clause allowing parties to terminate the relationship if the results from the preliminary testing are unsatisfactory.

**Unsatisfactory Test Results**

**Termination upon Unsatisfactory Results.** If any of the results of the medical or drug testing, or the mental health counseling is unsatisfactory to any of the parties, this agreement will terminate with no further obligations due or owing by or to any of the parties.

## E. MEDICAL PROCEDURES AND BEHAVIOR RESTRICTIONS

The last section discussed preliminary medical testing and mental health counseling. If any of those results make proceeding imprudent, then the surrogacy arrangement will terminate. If, however, all goes well with the testing and mental health evaluations, then the parties will proceed to the next stage. This next stage involves the medical procedures related to the impregnation, pregnancy, and the birth of the child.

### 1) Medical Procedures and Assumption of Risk

Once the preliminary testing is done, almost all of the medical procedures and obligations are those of the surrogate. In this stage there are no parallel commitments for the intended parents. Instead, the surrogate agrees to follow a medication regime to prepare her for the embryo transfer, and then agree to the actual embryo transfer, any resulting pregnancy, and the birthing process. The intended parents will likely want to know that the surrogate does acknowledge the risks of those procedures and will not hold them responsible for those risks.

One of the variables involved in the procedure is how many embryos the parties are willing to transfer to the surrogate. Since success rates for IVF are often lower than fifty percent, many intended parents transfer two or three embryos into the surrogate in hopes that at least one will be successful. Of course, the risk of transferring two or three embryos is becoming pregnant with multiple fetuses, a high-risk situation for both the surrogate and the fetuses. As a result, this is an issue that the parties need to discuss.

Parties should consult with their physician on how many embryos it is prudent to transfer. This amount may also depend on the success rate at that particular clinic and for situations like the one involving this particular surrogate and intended parents.

It is not uncommon for parties to leave this decision until the day when the transfer will happen.

If the embryos are very high quality, then the parties will generally transfer fewer, maybe just one. Since the number depends on the viability of the embryos, parties usually agree that they will transfer "up to" a certain number of embryos and fewer if the responsible physician advises otherwise.

The number of embryos the parties want to transfer is a good example of an issue that the parties may not consider unless prompted to do so through the negotiation of a surrogacy agreement. If the parties cannot agree on this issue, it is better for them to part ways early on in the process, and for the intended parents to seek another surrogate.

**Submission to Medical Procedures**

**Medical Procedures.** The Surrogate agrees to receive the transfer of [only one embryo] [up to a maximum of two embryos] [up to a maximum of three embryos] created through IVF and then, if a pregnancy results, to carry the resulting fetus(es) to term and to deliver them under the direction of a Responsible Physician. The Surrogate further agrees to cooperate fully with any Responsible Physician to assure that these procedures have the highest chance of success.

**Assumed Risks.** The Surrogate [and her spouse] acknowledge[s] that she [they] understand[s] the medical and psychological risks associated with these procedures, including in the extreme, the possibility of her death due to complications, and agree[s] not to hold the Intended Parent[s] responsible for any of those risks.

## 2) Behavioral Restrictions

Beyond agreeing to undergo the procedures, the surrogate also will need to acknowledge that she will be required to restrict her behavior in order to ensure a successful embryo transfer procedure and pregnancy so that any children born have the best chance of being healthy. This means that at the beginning stage of embryo transfer, the surrogate might well be asked to refrain from sexual intercourse of any sort for a certain amount of time before and just after the transfer. This ensures that any baby born is the result of the transferred embryos.

Additional restrictions throughout the process include the surrogate refraining from drinking alcohol or using certain drugs or amphetamines. Amphetamines may include prescription medications. If the surrogate takes any of these medications, then the parties will need to discuss the situation with their physician. It is possible that in that situation, the intended parents will want to work with a different surrogate.

Having these conversations early on in the process may save the parties time and energy. Parties may also want to include a clause that clearly states the consequences of violating the behavioral restrictions. These consequences may include termination of the agreement.

However, if the surrogate is already pregnant when the violation occurs, then the intended parents will probably not want to terminate the agreement as they will likely still want to take parental rights to any child born. In this situation there may be financial penalties for the surrogate. The intended parents need to have flexibility to make the decision about what to do if the surrogate violates the behavioral restrictions. As a result, the agreement may specify that any violation of the behavioral restrictions represents a material breach of the agreement by the surrogate and would give the intended parents the option to terminate their obligations under the agreement or reduce the amount of their payment obligations.[4]

**Behavioral Restrictions**

**Behavioral Restrictions.** The Surrogate also agrees to follow the behavioral guidelines of any Responsible Physician in order to assure the highest degree of success with the procedures. This includes taking any medication as it is prescribed, attending appointments, allowing testing and blood draws. It also includes refraining from sexual intercourse for [two weeks] before and [two weeks] after the embryo transfer. It further includes refraining from behavior that could harm the Child. This includes smoking cigarettes, drinking alcohol or taking certain proscribed drugs throughout the process, beginning [two weeks] before the embryo transfer and extending through to childbirth. After the

[4] The intended parents should try to avoid this situation through careful assessment of the surrogate. It is still important for drafters to include a clause in the contract that covers the behavioral restrictions.

> [28th] week of pregnancy, the surrogate also agrees not to undertake any significant travel away from her home, including not flying. Any violation of this provision will be deemed a material breach of the agreement by the surrogate and will allow the Intended Parents the option to terminate their obligations hereunder or to reduce payments as they deem reasonable.

Behavioral restrictions have been discussed above in connection with any abortion decision. These kinds of behavioral restrictions do represent a limitation on the personal liberty of the surrogate. Accordingly, it is not entirely clear whether they would be legally enforceable or not. Nonetheless, getting all the parties to discuss their expectations for the behavior of the surrogate during the course of the surrogacy arrangement may well result in the surrogate living up to those expectations voluntarily. Even having the discussions may result in the parties either discovering that they have shared values and expectations, or finding that they may not want to work together. Legally, while enforcement of behavioral restrictions is unclear, where they are reasonable and agreed to, they may well be enforceable.

### 3) Committing to a Certain Number of Embryo Transfer Cycles

The parties may also want to include in the contract what will happen if an embryo transfer does not result in a pregnancy. This includes whether they want to work together to attempt another cycle and how many cycles are they willing to commit to.

Intended parents may not want to invest their time and energy into a relationship with a surrogate who is only willing to attempt one cycle. With success rates of IVF often lower than fifty percent, several cycles may be necessary before a successful pregnancy is achieved.

Accordingly, it is common for parties to agree up front that they will undertake at least two or three cycles until a successful pregnancy is achieved. Alternatively, parties can enter into a new agreement or extend their old one if they want to continue with a new cycle after an unsuccessful one.

Going through a cycle helps parties get to know each other, and either the surrogate or the intended parents may end up not wanting to go through another cycle with their current counterpart. It may, therefore, be best to see how the first cycle transpires before committing to additional cycles. If both parties are still happy after the first cycle so that they want to go through a second or even third cycle, then they can agree to continue at that point.

**Tales from the Field: Behavioral Violations and Number of Cycles**

With our second surrogate, we had committed in our surrogacy agreement to work together for at least two embryo transfer cycles. The first cycle was abandoned because the surrogate did not regularly take the medications as prescribed by the physician and consequently her uterine lining had not thickened sufficiently to allow for a successful transfer. She confessed that she was so sure she would be pregnant that she took a cruise with her husband where they "partied all week"—smoking, drinking cocktails, and often sleeping in late, resulting in several missed medication dosages. As a result, we, as the intended parents, decided not to work with that surrogate for a second cycle.

At that point, the surrogate demanded that we continue to work with her for another cycle since we had agreed to that in our contract. We did not, however, since we viewed the surrogate's behavior as a breach of her behavior obligations, voiding any further obligation on our part.

If the parties decide that they want to commit to at least two cycles in advance, then the contract language needs to reflect this decision. It might also include clear language that embarking on a second embryo transfer would be contingent on the good faith behavior of each of the parties during the first cycle.

**Number of Cycles**

**Number of Cycles.** The parties agree to work together through a second embryo transfer cycle if the first embryo transfer cycle does not result in a successful pregnancy, provided that each of the parties acted in good faith and in accord with the terms of this agreement during the first cycle.

## F. PREGNANCY INSTRUCTIONS AND WHO CAN DECIDE

This section will address some of the controversial issues that are specifically related to what can happen during the pregnancy. These issues are complicated and uncomfortable for most people to think about and discuss. It is for exactly that reason that they must be addressed in advance, and their inclusion in the draft agreement will prompt the conversation. As with other controversial areas, if the surrogate and the intended parents cannot agree on these provisions, it may be best for the parties not to work together.

### 1) Possible Termination of the Pregnancy

The parties must confront whether and when they would want to terminate a pregnancy. It is crucial that the parties agree on this because courts cannot compel a surrogate to have an abortion. Thus, if the intended parents believe that in certain circumstances they would want to terminate the pregnancy, then they need to be able to make that decision and have the surrogate follow their wishes. Even if the terms of that particular behavioral agreement are not specifically enforceable by courts, including the expectations of the parties in the agreement serves as a prompt for their conversation about the possibility of terminating the pregnancy. It also helps make sure the parties are all in agreement about possible termination of the pregnancy, such that the surrogate would likely agree voluntarily if the discussed circumstances arise.

Now that *Roe v. Wade* has been overturned by the United States Supreme Court, each state in the United States has its own abortion laws. A growing list of states in the United States including Texas and Wisconsin now have a total or near total ban on abortion. Other states, like California, Illinois, and New York, still permit abortion through the second trimester. No agreement about abortion among the parties to a surrogacy agreement will enable a surrogate to have an abortion if it is illegal in her state at her stage of pregnancy. So, once again, if abortion is an option you would like to have in certain circumstances, you'll need to check with your attorney about the abortion restrictions in your surrogate's state. You may end up wanting to work with a surrogate in a state that is relatively permissive with regard to abortion.

If the surrogate expresses some hesitation about following the termination wishes of the intended parents, then the intended parents may want to work with a different surrogate. This may avoid the chance that the surrogate's hesitation develops into full-blown resistance after three months of pregnancy. If the surrogate does not terminate the pregnancy, at least one of the intended parents likely will still be the biological parent and will likely be responsible for child support for any child born even if the intended parents attempt to refuse to take parental responsibility.

If the intended parents would never want to terminate a pregnancy under any circumstances, then they need to make sure that their surrogate agrees with them. Their surrogate should be prepared to carry a child through to childbirth even if it may have severe birth defects or other extreme medical conditions.

The surrogate will also need to be sure that the intended parents share her views about terminating a pregnancy. If she would not want to abort a pregnancy under any circumstance, then she will likely not want to work with intended parents who would want her to have an abortion, even if it is only under certain limited circumstances.

There are rare occasions when continuing a pregnancy would put the surrogate's life at risk. If this is the case, then generally the parties will defer to the surrogate to make the decision about whether to proceed with or terminate the pregnancy.

| **Possible Termination of the Pregnancy** |
| --- |
| **Terminating the Pregnancy.** The parties hereto agree that because any Child born will be the Child of the Intended Parent(s), that the Intended Parent(s) can make a decision to terminate the pregnancy [for any reason] [only if there are certain extreme medical circumstances] up until the [12th] [20th] week of pregnancy, as measured from the date of insemination. Understanding that such provision is not specifically enforceable, the Surrogate agrees to follow the wishes of the Intended Parent(s) in this regard. |

> In any event, the parties agree that if any Responsible Physician advises that continuing the pregnancy puts the Surrogate's life or health at risk, then the Surrogate shall have the right to decide to terminate the pregnancy at any time.

### 2) Selective Reduction

Another important issue to address is whether the parties would agree to a selective reduction in the event that the surrogate becomes pregnant with multiples. Such a pregnancy is risky for the surrogate and the fetuses, and raising multiple children is considerably more difficult for the intended parents.

This discussion is closely related to the discussion of how many embryos to transfer. There is an increased risk of multiples with more embryos that are transferred. However, even the transfer of one embryo could end up in multiples if that embryo splits. If the intended parents and the surrogate are not comfortable with multiples, then they should consider only transferring one embryo.

One approach to managing multiples is to only perform a selective reduction if there are three or more developing embryos. This is not likely if only transferring one or two embryos in the first place, but it is still possible if embryos split.

If there are three or more developing embryos, then the parties may agree only to terminate those embryos that have the lowest chance of survival, as determined by a responsible physician, and allow two to remain and develop. The parties need to discuss their intentions to make sure they agree on what to do if there are multiples.

In addition, a prudent drafter will include a provision explaining that selective reduction may also occur if the life or health of the surrogate is at risk. This is similar to the provision included in the termination of pregnancy clause discussed above. These kinds of provisions are designed to protect the health and safety of the surrogate, but also to remind the intended parents of the potential for termination of a pregnancy if the health of the surrogate is indeed at risk.

| **Selective Reduction** |
|---|
| **Selective Reduction.** The parties hereto agree that if the Surrogate becomes pregnant with [two] [three] or more embryos, that the Intended Parent(s) will have the right to request a selective reduction up until the [12th][20th] week of pregnancy, as measured from the date of insemination. If such a request is made, then the Responsible Physician will identify the embryos with the lowest chance of survival and will terminate that or those embryos, allowing the most viable to remain and develop. Understanding that such a provision is not specifically enforceable, the Surrogate agrees to respect and follow the wishes of the Intended Parent(s) in this regard. |

> In any event, the parties agree that if any Responsible Physician advises that continuing to be pregnant with multiples puts the Surrogate's life or health at risk, then the Surrogate shall have the right to decide to terminate any or all of the embryos at any time.

## G. BIRTH PROCEDURES, RIGHTS, AND OBLIGATIONS

After discussing the preliminary testing and issues related to the pregnancy, the next stage to consider is the actual birthing of the child and the separation of the child from the surrogate at birth. It is in connection with this stage that the parties should affirm the intended parents' commitment to acknowledge full parental responsibility and take custody. The surrogate should likewise agree that neither she nor her partner or spouse, if there is one, will attempt to assert any parental rights or to take custody. Those affirmations are at the crux of the surrogacy relationship and their importance cannot be minimized.

This section may also contemplate issues like what to do in the rare event that a child born is not related to the intended parents or not related to any of the parties at all. Finally, the drafter may also include provisions addressing what may happen if the intended parents separate or if one or both of the intended parents die during the pregnancy and before the birth.

### 1) Intended Parents Affirmation of Parental Rights and Custody

Central to the surrogacy arrangement is the intended parents' commitment to take full parental responsibility and custody of any child born. There is a risk that a surrogate will attempt to assert parental rights and take custody of any child born as shown in the *Baby M* and *Baby Boy A* cases. Most surrogates, however, are worried that the intended parents may change their minds and not want any child born so that the surrogate will feel compelled to raise that child or children. It is crucial for parties to discuss all of the possibilities and be absolutely certain that the intended parents are committed to raising the child or children. This also means that parties need to contemplate the notion that a child born may actually have health concerns, birth defects, or a debilitating disease.

The logical conclusion of the intended parents having full parental rights upon birth is that they also have the unfettered right to make medical decisions on behalf of their child immediately at birth. This is not necessarily legally the case. Parties need to address this in the agreement since, in many states, the surrogate, as a birth mother, will be considered to be the legal mother until a court rules otherwise. This means that the surrogate might have the legal right to make healthcare decisions for any child she delivers.

**Intended Parent(s) Responsible for Child**

**Intended Parent(s) Commit(s) to Full Parental Responsibility.** The Intended Parent(s) commit(s) to take full parental responsibility and custody of any child born through the surrogacy process immediately upon the birth of such child. This commitment shall be unwavering, regardless of any medical condition or affliction that may affect any such child.

Surrogate [and her partner or spouse] agree(s) not to assert any claim to parental rights or custody and agrees to cooperate to the fullest extent to support and enforce the parental rights of the Intended Parent(s), including cooperating in any necessary legal proceedings.

**Intended Parent(s) Make(s) All Medical Decisions After Birth.** Accordingly, the Intended Parent(s) shall also have the full and absolute right to make any medical decisions on behalf of any such child immediately upon their birth. Surrogate [and her partner or spouse] agree(s) to cooperate to the fullest extent to make sure that Intended Parent(s) (has) (have) those full and absolute rights, including executing a medical power of attorney in their favor if necessary.

### 2) Child Born Unrelated to Intended Parents

The agreement should also address what the parties would do if any child born to the surrogate through the process is not actually genetically related to the intended parents. The parties need to discuss this so that they know the actions they would take in this circumstance. The risk of this happening may also make the parties more carefully follow the medical protocols designed to ensure that any child born is indeed a child of the intended parents.

For example, the parties may agree that if the child is not related to the intended parents, but is genetically linked to the surrogate, then the surrogate would have the first right to parent the child and the intended parents would have no obligation to assert parental rights.

If the child is not genetically linked to either the intended parents or the surrogate, as the case would be if the incorrect embryos were implanted in the surrogate, then the parties may agree that the intended parents would have the first right to become the legal parents of the child, but would not be obligated to do so. If the intended parents decline that option, then the surrogate would have the option to assert her legal parental rights. If neither the intended parents nor the surrogate wants to be a legal parent, then the child could be put up for adoption. Below are sample clauses that contemplate the situation where the child is unrelated to the intended parents.

| **Unrelated Child** |
| --- |
| Child Born Unrelated to Intended Parent(s).<br>(a) If, after relevant medical tests, it is determined that any child born is not |

genetically related to the Intended Parent(s), then the Intended Parent(s) shall be under no obligation to assume any parental rights over such child.

(b) In such a case described in paragraph (a), if the child is genetically linked to the Surrogate, then the Surrogate shall have the first option to assume her parental rights and take custody of the child. If the Surrogate declines that option, then the Intended Parent(s) may choose to adopt the child and the Surrogate agrees to cooperate fully with that choice. If the Intended Parent(s) do not so choose, then the child may be put up for adoption by a third party.

(c) If the child is not genetically linked to any of the parties, then the Intended Parent(s) will have the first option to adopt the child and the Surrogate agrees to cooperate fully with that choice. If the Intended Parent(s) decline that option, then the Surrogate may choose to adopt the child. If the Surrogate does not so choose, then the child may be put up for adoption by a third party.

### 3) Changed Circumstances for the Intended Parents

The parties need to discuss and come to an agreement concerning what would happen if there is a change of circumstances with the intended parents.[5] If the intended parents are a couple, they may separate or divorce during the course of the surrogacy arrangement. Alternatively, one or both of the intended parents may die.

For example, if a couple splits up, then the intended parents will need to specify which of them would to remain the sole intended parent. If one of the intended parents is genetically linked to the child, then that person would likely be the sole intended parent, but it is up the intended parents to decide on that.

If one of the intended parents dies, then the other would likely want to remain the sole intended parent. However, if both of the intended parents die, then the intended parents must specify who will become the legal guardian or parents of the child born through the process. Thinking through these possibilities, like so many of the uncomfortable issues described already, helps the parties understand what they would do if that unthinkable circumstance occurred.

---

[5] *See* Tamar Lewin, *Surrogates and Couples Face a Maze of Laws, State by State*, N.Y. TIMES (Sept. 18, 2014), https://www.nytimes.com/2014/09/18/us/surrogates-and-couples-face-a-maze-of-laws-state-by-state.html?searchResultPosition=1 (citing Andrew W. Vorzimer, a surrogacy lawyer, who said that intended parents remarkably often change their minds during the surrogacy arrangement).

| **Change in Intended Parents' Circumstances** |
|---|
| Changed Circumstances for the Intended Parent(s).<br>(a) [Paragraphs (a) and (b) here are only applicable if the intended parents are part of a couple.] If the Intended Parents separate or divorce during the course of the surrogacy arrangement, but before the birth of the child, then the sole Intended Parent shall be A. [This is because it is A who will be genetically linked to the child.]<br>(b) If one of the intended parents dies, then the sole intended parent shall be the surviving intended parent.<br>(c) If [both intended parents die] [the intended parent dies], then the intended parent[s] want[s] to make known [his] [her] [their] intention that parental rights and custody be vested in [the chosen person or couple. That person or couple] has discussed this matter with the Intended Parents and has agreed to become the parent or parents of any child born in such event. [Consider having that person or couple sign this agreement to acknowledge this undertaking.] |

## H. FINANCIAL ISSUES, INCLUDING INSURANCE

The financial issues are likely to be paramount in each of the parties' minds. The intended parents are concerned due to the high overall cost of surrogacy, and they will likely want to keep those costs within what they are able to pay. The surrogate cares about financial issues because compensation is one of the reasons why she is agreeing to be a surrogate in the first place. This is not to undermine the altruism inherent in being a surrogate, but, in short, money matters.

### 1) Base Compensation

Typically, there is a base compensation that the intended parents will pay to the surrogate. Currently, base compensation in the United States can range from $20,000 to $70,000 or more. Some surrogates do not charge at all because they are a friend or relative of the intended parents while others may charge more if they are able to negotiate for a higher amount. Agencies may well have a pre-determined rate of pay for the surrogates they recruit and provide. If there is not a pre-determined base compensation for the surrogate, the parties will negotiate an amount that makes them all comfortable, or perhaps all slightly uncomfortable, with the intended parents feeling like they are paying somewhat more than they would like, and the surrogate feeling like she is getting slightly less than she would like.

Crucial to the discussion of base compensation, however, is the timing of the compensation. The intended parents do not want to pay a large portion of the fee unless the pregnancy is viable. As a result, compensation is generally paid over a period of time, with smaller amounts paid in the initial phases and larger amounts paid as the pregnancy continues. The surrogate often does not receive a significant amount of the money until the successful delivery of one or more children.

Naturally, delayed compensation is not ideal for the surrogate. The surrogate will be going through major medical treatments early and throughout the pregnancy and may argue that she should be paid at least as much in the early stages as later on in the process. Moreover, if the pregnancy is not successful, the surrogate will not receive very much for her efforts if early payments are small. Thus, the parties will need to negotiate a payment schedule that seems fair to all parties.

The payment schedule should be keyed to clear milestones so that all of the parties understand when payment is due. If the intended parents are paying the surrogate through an escrow account, then the escrow agent who will disburse the payments needs to know exactly when amounts are due. The sample language below presents one possible schedule for payments.

| Base Compensation |
| --- |
| **Base Compensation.** The Intended Parent(s) agree to pay Surrogate for her services a base compensation of [$50,000].<br><br>**Timing of Base Compensation Payments.** The base compensation is payable according to the following schedule: |

$2,000—at the start of medications preparing surrogate for embryo transfer;

$2,000—at the time of embryo transfer;

$5,000—at confirmation of a viable pregnancy at 12 weeks after embryo transfer;

$5,000—every four weeks thereafter, provided that the pregnancy is still viable;

The remaining balance due will be payable upon the successful delivery of one or more children who survive childbirth.

### 2) Expense and Reimbursement Payments

Parties often focus on and negotiate the base compensation for the surrogate and spend surprisingly little time on the other costs and expenses that should rightly be paid by the intended parents. The surrogate will need to make sure that, in addition to her base compensation, any and all out-of-pocket expenses related to the surrogacy arrangement are paid for, or reimbursed by, the intended parents. The intended parents, by contrast, will want to include a limit on those expenses to ensure that they are manageable. The sample language below covers expenses and reimbursements.

**Expenses and Reimbursements**

**Expense and Reimbursement Payments.** The Intended Parent(s) also agree to pay directly, if possible, or else to reimburse Surrogate for, any and all out-of-pocket expenses related to the surrogacy arrangement that are not covered by any applicable insurance. These expenses include, but are not limited to, expenses for:

- medical testing;
- mental health evaluation;
- any medications or vitamins recommended or required by any Responsible Physician;
- [if Surrogate has other children] any childcare required by surrogate to facilitate her service and attendance at appointments, not to exceed a total of [$1,000];
- reasonable costs for maternity clothes, not to exceed a total of [$1,000]; and
- any actual lost wages resulting from work surrogate is required to miss because of the pregnancy (as certified by any Responsible Physician), not to exceed [$5,000].

Timing of Expense and Reimbursement Payments. Any such expense or reimbursement payment is due at the time when it is incurred.

### 3) Additional Compensation

The parties should think through the financial implications of any complications that may arise during the course of the pregnancy, like carrying multiples, having a miscarriage, or a mandatory Cesarean section for the delivery. These complications also include any health problems that the surrogate may acquire as a result of the surrogate agreeing to help the intended parents. The intended parents should expect to assist the surrogate with additional compensation if those complications arise. The sample clauses below address additional compensation for the surrogate.

| **Additional Compensation** |
|---|
| **Additional Compensation.** Intended Parent(s) shall provide thee Surrogate with additional compensation in the following amounts for the events listed: |
| \$5,000—for an abortion requested by the Intended Parents, or recommended or required by any Responsible Physician; |
| \$5,000—for any selective reduction requested by the Intended Parents or recommended or required by any Responsible Physician; |
| \$5,000—for a Cesarian section recommended or required by any Responsible Physician; |
| \$10,000—for each additional child beyond one if there are multiple live births; |
| \$10,000—for a partial or full hysterectomy recommended or required by any Responsible Physician as a result of the surrogacy. |
| Timing of Additional Compensation. Any such compensation is due to Surrogate whenever the event that triggers the compensation occurs. |

All of these expenses can be quite significant, and potentially exceed an additional \$10,000 or more.

The intended parents will want to review all of these provisions closely to make sure that they are comfortable with these additional payments if incurred.

### 4) Escrow Arrangements

Parties may want to establish a payment system that involves an escrow account managed by an escrow agent. That account will be funded in advance by the intended parents. This reassures the surrogate that the costs will be covered and paid when due. The escrow agent will make payments from that account upon proof that the payment is due. Any amount remaining in the account at the conclusion of the surrogacy arrangement will revert back to the intended parents.

The downside to the escrow arrangement is that it adds an additional layer of complexity to the relationship between the surrogate and the intended parents. There will also be a fee associated with establishing and maintaining an escrow account of approximately $1,000 or more, though it might be a service that a surrogacy agency provides as part of their overall fee.

If an escrow arrangement is desired, the parties will likely need to negotiate and execute a more detailed escrow agreement. This process will take time and increase the attorneys' fees. The money put into escrow should be sufficient to cover all the potential costs of the intended parents, including expenses, reimbursements, and additional compensation that may become due. The sample provision below addresses the use of an escrow account.

| Possible Escrow |
| --- |
| **Escrow.** The parties agree to establish an escrow account that will be managed by X, as the escrow agent. The Intended Parent(s) will fund the escrow account with [$100,000] to cover any and all possible payments to surrogate. The escrow agent will make disbursements from the escrow account to the Surrogate when presented with proof that the amount is due and owing. The escrow agent will notify the intended parents of any such disbursement, giving them 5 business days to contest such payment before payment is actually made. Any fees associated with the escrow will be payable by Intended Parent(s). |

### 5) Medical and Life Insurance

Insurance can help cover the medical costs and expenses associated with surrogacy. However, many insurance policies do not cover surrogacy. In this case, the intended parents may opt to pay all of the costs and expenses themselves. Of course, there is a risk that the expenses will skyrocket if there are any extraordinary medical complications.

#### *a) Insurance Covering Surrogacy*

To address this situation, there are now insurance companies that offer medical coverage that helps pay for the medical costs and expenses incurred by a surrogate, including amounts triggered by extraordinary medical complications. The cost for that kind of insurance is currently roughly around $25,000 to $35,000 for a single pregnancy, or $40,000–$50,000 for twins.[6] That amount may actually be more than the out-of-pocket expenses associated with a routine pregnancy and delivery. Still, the intended parents may wish to consider purchasing a policy to cover themselves in the event of extraordinary medical expenses.

### *b) Life Insurance*

In addition, it is now common for surrogates to request that intended parent(s) purchase life insurance that would cover the life of the surrogate and pay her family in the event of her death. While death is highly unlikely, life insurance gives the surrogate added comfort that insurance would help provide for her family if she were to die.

| **Insurance and Medical Expenses** |
| --- |
| **Insurance and Medical Expenses.** The Intended Parents will purchase a Health Insurance Policy, which will cover the Surrogate for major medical procedures or treatments and any hospitalizations related to her pregnancy and the delivery of any child pursuant to the surrogacy arrangement. Intended Parents also agree to pay any medical expenses related to the Surrogate's pregnancy and the delivery of any child pursuant |

[6] *See, e.g., Surrogacy Maternity Insurance Coverage Options*, ART RISK, https://artrisksolutions.com/surrogacy-maternity-insurance-options/ (last visited June 18, 2023).

> to the surrogacy arrangement that are not covered by insurance.
>
> The Intended Parents will also purchase a Life Insurance Policy for the Surrogate, which will cover the life of the surrogate and will pay her family, in the unfortunate event of her death, [$1,000,000].
>
> Intended Parents will keep the Health Insurance Policy and the Life Insurance Policy in effect throughout the surrogacy arrangement up until [sixteen] weeks after the birth of any child pursuant to the surrogacy arrangement.

## I. MISCELLANEOUS PROVISIONS

Finally, as with any contract, there are boilerplate provisions that are typically found at the end of the contract. Most of these provisions are not worth negotiating and are not unique to a surrogacy arrangement. For example, there will likely be a severability clause, meaning any unenforceable provisions of the agreement will be severed from the rest of the agreement so that the rest of the agreement remains in force. There will also likely be a provision simply identifying addresses of the parties for purposes of any communications. As straightforward as these provisions are, the parties should read all of the boilerplate clauses and discuss them with their attorney to make sure they understand the implications of each. However, some so-called boilerplate provisions are unique to surrogacy and are worth considering here.

### 1) Choice of Law and Venue

The vital importance of expressly choosing a surrogacy supportive state law to govern your surrogacy arrangement was discussed in Chapter 4. Accordingly, a section about which state's law will govern the parties' agreement should be included in these provisions. Choice-of-law provisions are important in most contracts, but vital in surrogacy arrangements with surrogacy arrangements since not all jurisdictions support and enforce surrogacy agreements. Just be sure to review your choice-of-law with your attorney to ensure that there are sufficient connections with the state whose law is chosen such that the choice will be honored by the courts.

In addition to the choice-of-law provision, a contract can contain a choice-of-venue provision. Parties should expressly agree that certain courts should and can take jurisdiction over any dispute arising under the contract. With a surrogacy arrangement, the courts of the place where the birth will occur should take jurisdiction over the matter. The sample clause below addresses choice-of-law and venue issues.

| Choice of Law and Venue |
| --- |
| **Choice of Law and Venue.** The parties hereto agree that this agreement, its validity, interpretation, and performance and any other disputes hereunder will be subject to the laws of [Illinois]. The parties also agree to submit their dispute to the [courts of Illinois]. |

## 2) Confidentiality

The parties may each have their own wishes with regard to whether or not the surrogacy arrangement is disclosed to others. The intended parents may want to control whether and when to discuss the surrogacy arrangement with their child or children born from the process. The surrogate also may or may not want to be known to the child or children born for fear of being more involved in their lives than she wants to be. These issues need to be discussed between the parties and their understanding should be set forth in the agreement.

Attorneys need to draft the provision according to the parties' specific needs. Below is one sample provision, but, as with all of the samples set forth here, it is not appropriate for all situations, and the parties should work with their attorney to make sure their intentions are reflected accurately in their agreement.

| Confidentiality |
| --- |
| **Confidentiality.** The Intended Parent(s) agree not to disclose the identity of the Surrogate to any third party, including any child born from the process, without her consent. Likewise, the Surrogate agrees not to disclose the identity of the Intended Parents with any third party without their consent. Notwithstanding the foregoing, the parties acknowledge that this provision does not apply to disclosures made to any of the professionals involved in the surrogacy process [or |

any other specific individuals the parties may want to name].

As you have seen, the surrogacy agreement is a roadmap for the surrogacy arrangement. It contains the commitments of the parties on a wide array of issues central to that arrangement. While understanding, discussing and negotiating through the entire lengthy agreement can seem daunting, it is crucial. Working through the issues and arriving at a mutually acceptable arrangement before any issues arise should help prevent conflicts down the road, and help ensure a positive relationship among the parties. The ultimate goal, of course, is that the parties are able to work together successfully to help the intended parents form or expand their family.

# CHAPTER 8
# THE EGG DONOR

For many intended parent(s) having biologically related children through surrogacy is only possible with the help of an egg donor. Sometimes egg donors are truly just women who are giving their eggs to the intended parent(s) altruistically to help them become parents. That might be the case where someone's sister or another relative or a friend is the egg donor.

But in many cases the term donor is a misnomer, and the egg donors are providing their eggs for compensation.[1] As with surrogacy, though, egg donors report that compensation is only one of the reasons why they do it. They also generally are excited to help others form their families. Indeed, studies of the motivations for egg donors have routinely found that altruism is one of the chief motivating factors for egg donors.[2]

## 1. EGG DONOR STORIES

| **Tales from the Field: A Super Donor** |
|---|
| One egg donor recounted having donated for seven different sets of intended parents and having had seven sets of twin boys as a result. |

[1] Wynter K. Miller, *Assumption of What? Building Better Market Architecture for Egg Donation*, 86 TENN. L. REV. 33, 38 (2018).

[2] *Id.* at 46–47.

She herself had three boys of her own with her husband. When I spoke with her, she was in the process of what she described as her last donation and was donating to a same sex couple from another country.

When asked how she felt about having been the biological mother to seventeen boys, she responded with a bit of a grin. "I know it seems weird, and in some ways it is true that I am biologically linked to seventeen boys, but I don't really consider the boys born from my donations to be my children. They are truly the children of their intended parents, and I simply helped those parents to have them."

She had worked through an agency to connect with her intended parents but felt very strongly that what she and the agency were doing was all about helping people start or build their families and not about the money involved. In fact, in at least one situation when the intended parents did not get pregnant with her first donation, she was prepared to donate again and waive any fee. However, those intended parents decided to try a different donor in hopes of increasing their chances of success.

In the first seven donations this egg donor was anonymous. The intended parents had seen her profile and pictures, but never knew her name or how to contact her. Likewise, she did not know the names or contact information of her intended parents.

But for the last donation she was proceeding as an "open donor." In other words, she was being open about who she is to the intended parents, and they are open with her about who they are. She was particularly excited about this situation, as getting to know the intended parents has made her even more excited and satisfied about her ability to help them realize their family formation dreams.

When I spoke with her, she was thirty-one and was pretty sure that she would only do one more egg donation. Interestingly, though, she did say that she was considering the possibility of being a surrogate.

There is some limit to these results, however, as there are not many empirical studies focusing on the motivations of egg donors. There is also some skepticism that egg donors may well be echoing the altruism narrative put forth and preferred by egg donation and surrogacy clinics.[3]

One very thorough examination of the motivations of egg donors found a range of motivations depending on the circumstances.[4] Donors who knew their intended parents were more likely to be motivated chiefly by altruism, but even commercial donors

---

[3] Rene Almeling, *Selling Genes, Selling Gender: Egg Agencies, Sperm Banks, and the Medical Market in Genetic Material*, 72 AM. SOCIO. REV. 319, 326 (2007).

[4] S. Purewal & O.B.A. van den Akker, *Systematic Review of Oocyte Donation: Investigating Attitudes, Motivations and Experiences*, 15 HUM. REPROD. UPDATE 499, 512 (2009), https://academic.oup.com/humupd/article/15/5/499/635693.

reported altruistic motivations in combination with financial ones.[5]

There are also some demographic and personal characteristics shared by many egg donors. Generally, egg donors are young and intelligent.[6] Most are in their twenties or early thirties, when a women's eggs are most viable.[7] Egg donors are specifically being recruited for their physical characteristics, their intelligence, their educational background, and any demonstrated athletic or other special abilities.[8]

Regardless of your motivations, if you are interested in becoming an egg donor and are eligible, or if you are an intended parent who will need the help of an egg donor, then this chapter should help you better understand what is entailed in the egg donation arrangement. This chapter will cover: the details of the process, critiques often made of egg donation, and finally a discussion of how to navigate legal and regulatory matters.

---

5 *Id.*

6 Miller, *supra* note 1, at 43.

7 Danielle A. Vera, *R-egg-ulation: A Call for Greater Regulation of the Big Business of Human Egg Harvesting*, 23 MICH. J. GENDER & L. 391, 398 (2016). *See also Understanding Ovulation & Fertility: Facts to Help You Get Pregnant,* reviewed by Dr. Brunilda Nazario, WEBMD: GROW (NOV. 15, 2021), https://www.webmd.com/baby/ss/slideshow-understanding-fertility-ovulation#1.

8 Miller, *supra* note 1, at 43–46.

## 2. THE EGG DONATION PROCESS

If you are interested in becoming an egg donor, you will want to understand the process that is involved. First, many egg donors work through an egg donation or surrogacy agency. That can make it easier for an egg donor to be matched with intended parent(s).

One of the issues any prospective egg donor should consider is whether to proceed in an anonymous or open donation. In an open donation the intended parents know who the egg donor is.

Many egg donors would prefer that the intended parent(s) not know their exact identity and contact information. In that way, the egg donor can limit her involvement in the family formation process to strictly and only the egg donation.

In an anonymous donation, not only should there be no ongoing financial or parental responsibilities for any children born, there should not be any contact between the egg donor and the intended parent(s). Moreover, there should be no contact between any children born from the egg donation and the egg donor.

There are exceptions to this anonymity. If the donor agrees, she may allow future contact in rare cases where any children born from the egg donation might need to know more about the medical history of the donor or her family, or may need to find a matching candidate for any possible tissue or organ transplants.

Generally, however, an anonymous egg donation will remain just that—anonymous. An agency is vital to this process as some intermediary is required to match anonymous egg donors with intended parent(s).

Assuming the egg donor works through an agency of some sort, perhaps even a fertility clinic, she will be asked to create a profile about herself. That profile will include a plethora of information about the egg donor, information that prospective intended parent(s) would want to know when selecting their egg donor. That background information may include, among other information:

- basic physical characteristics,
- age,
- educational background,
- athletic abilities,
- music abilities,
- artistic abilities,
- general medical history,
- whether the egg donor has had children,
- description of those children,
- whether the egg donor has had any miscarriages,
- family medical history including parents and siblings,
- existence of any genetic diseases in the family,

- pictures of the egg donor at various ages in her life,
- pictures of any children of the egg donor, and
- pictures of the egg donor's parents and siblings.

With all of this information in today's age of modern medical and technological capabilities, anonymous begins to sound dubious. Indeed, with DNA testing and facial recognition technology, any children born to a surrogate may well be able to find their egg donor without too much difficulty, even without going through the agency with an agreed upon reason for contacting the egg donor.

**Concerns over Anonymity**

Anyone considering becoming an egg donor may want to proceed anonymously to be certain that there will be no ongoing financial or parental obligations for any children born. But truly anonymous egg donations in a world of advanced medical and technological capabilities may not be possible to achieve.

The risk of children born through the egg donation some day attempting to contact their egg donor is something the egg donor will need to assess for herself.

This potential for breaching the anonymity of the egg donor is one of the reasons why the agreement of the parties is all the more important. A survey of the kinds of provisions that are in that agreement is contained in Chapter 9, but among those provisions will be an undertaking from the intended parents that they will only attempt contact with the egg donor in certain rare, limited, and agreed-upon circumstances.

One additional safeguard to prevent this is an undertaking by the intended parents to destroy any identifying information they have about the egg donor once the egg donation is complete. Policing that kind of an agreement, however, presents its own challenges. Intended parents may well want to keep that information specifically so that their children would have an easier ability to find their egg donor if the need or interest arises.

The egg donor also should recognize that any children born will not be parties to the egg donor agreement. So, the children themselves might someday search for their egg donor with no contractual limitations on their ability to do that. This is a risk that the egg donor will need to assess for herself. Perhaps an egg donor would not be troubled by a young adult contacting her so that they could meet their egg donor. At that stage, it's not likely that any financial or parental obligations would arise. But even tech-savvy teenagers might pursue contact with their egg donor. Again, egg donors will need to get comfortable with this possibility.

Once the egg donor and the intended parent(s) are matched they will work with lawyers to craft and finalize an egg donor agreement to memorialize the specific terms of their unique arrangement. That process is discussed in more details in the next section of this chapter, which focuses on the legal aspects of egg donation.

Assuming the parties come to a mutually acceptable agreement, the medical exams, treatments, and protocols will begin. The egg donor will need to have agreed to those procedures and acknowledged that there are always medical risks associated with those procedures.

| The Egg Donation Process |
|---|
| 1. The egg donor needs to assess the commitment and the related risks, and decide **that egg donation is right for her**; |
| 2. The egg donor likely will **contact an agency or fertility clinic** to facilitate the process; |
| 3. Decide whether donation will be **anonymous or open**; |
| 4. Find and **agree upon a fertility doctor** and clinic; |
| 5. Work with attorneys to **negotiate the egg donor contract** (typically a different attorney from the one representing the intended parent(s)); |
| 6. Assess **whether to procure insurance** to cover any medical complications; |
| 7. **Arrange for mental health evaluation** for the egg donor to understand and be prepared for the process, risks, and dynamics; |

8. **Begin medical health consultation** for the egg donor;
9. **Begin injectable medications for egg donor** to hyper-stimulate and regulate her ovaries in anticipation of egg retrieval; and
10. **Undergo surgical removal of eggs**.

There will likely be a threshold mental health consultation to ensure the egg donor fully understands the process and likely will be able to uphold her commitments that are a part of the arrangement. This is analogous to the mental health consultations that the surrogate and the intended parents will both likely undergo as well.

Assuming the mental health consultation is successful for the egg donor, the egg donor will then undergo physical examinations to determine her fitness for the egg donation process. The physical examinations will include drug testing and possibly genetic testing to screen the egg donor to see if she is a carrier of genes that may result in any genetic diseases.

If the initial mental and medical evaluations go well, the egg donor will be cleared for the donation. The agency or fertility clinic will coordinate the timing for the egg donation with the intended parent(s) and the surrogate to ensure the highest chances of success with the egg donation and the subsequent fertilization and then embryo transfer.

At the agreed upon time, the egg donor will begin a protocol of medications to facilitate the retrieval of multiple eggs.[9] All of this is done from the beginning to the end of one menstrual cycle. During this time, the egg donor will also need to refrain from using any contraception medication and should stop having intercourse as the chances of becoming pregnant will be magnified.

One of the medications, referred to as follicle stimulating hormones, is designed to hyper-stimulate the ovaries to produce multiple eggs.[10] Another one of the medications, Lupron, is designed to regulate her hormone levels and make sure the eggs aren't released from the ovaries prematurely in the process.[11] Yet another medication, human chorionic gonadotropin, given shortly before the egg retrieval, is designed to mature the eggs and get them ready to be removed.[12] These medications are generally injections.[13] So, the egg donor has to be prepared for that kind of treatment.

The actual egg retrieval involves a surgical procedure that is done with the egg donor under partial sedation. An ultrasound is used to guide the physician removing the eggs and a suctioning needle is inserted trans vaginally into the egg donor's ovaries to find and remove the eggs.[14]

---

[9] For a fairly detailed description of the egg donation process, *see id.* at 39–41.

[10] *Id.* at 40.

[11] *Id.* at 40–41.

[12] *Id.* at 40.

[13] *Id.* at 39–40.

[14] *Id.* at 41.

There are potential side effects to the medications and the medical procedures involved with egg donation. Some side effects are minor, including discomfort and mood swings from the hormone protocols.[15] But some side effects can be more serious and might, in rare cases be life threatening, including internal bleeding and other complications.[16] One study linked the use of gonadotropin to higher risks for colorectal cancer.[17] Anyone seriously considering becoming an egg donor should absolutely consult with their own medical specialist and assess the risks before deciding that egg donation is right for them.

**Medical Risks**

Anyone seriously considering becoming an egg donor should absolutely consult with their own medical specialist before deciding that egg donation is right for them. Agencies or others might make egg donation seem simple and lucrative. However, the process does involve multiple injectable medications to hyper-stimulate and regulate egg production, and then an invasive surgical procedure to remove the eggs.

Side effects can range from mild to, in rare cases, serious and even life threatening. Egg donors should educate themselves and consider these risks thoroughly before moving forward with any arrangement.

---

15 Kamakahi v. Am. Soc'y for Reprod. Med., 305 F.R.D. 164, 170 (N.D. Cal. 2015). *See also* Vera, *supra* note 7, at 397.

16 Vera, *supra* note 7, at 397.

17 *Id.*

## 3. CRITICISMS OF EGG DONATIONS

Similar to the criticisms of surrogacy, there are feminists, scholars, and commentators who are either opposed to or skeptical of egg donation.[18] The primary criticisms include the possibility that egg donations may not involve true and informed consent by the egg donor to the procedures and risks involved, and instead may result in exploitation and commodification.[19]

These concerns were also discussed in connection with surrogacy. They are at the core of why some jurisdictions have limited or prohibited both surrogacy and egg donations for compensation.

The arguments assume that the women who would consider becoming egg donors (or surrogates) would be at a financial disadvantage by comparison with the intended parents who tend to be older and more economically secure. That disadvantage might result in egg donors effectively agreeing to the arrangement without truly understanding its consequences. The result might be exploitation and even commodification, where the women involved, their eggs, and perhaps even the children born could be viewed as being bought and sold.

But other commentators argue that women, particularly in well developed markets like the United States, should be allowed the contractual and

---

18 Miller, *supra* note 1, at 54–55.

19 *See* Vera, *supra* note 7; Alana Cattapan, *Risky Business: Surrogacy, Egg Donation, and the Politics of Exploitation*, 29 No. 3 CAN. J.L. & SOC'Y 361 (2014); Miller, *supra* note 1.

reproductive autonomy to decide for themselves whether to participate in these types of arrangements. Indeed, presuming that women are not able to make these kinds of financial decisions relating to their reproductive ability is in itself paternalistic and demeaning. The Ethics Committee of the American Society for Reproductive Medicine (ASRM), having studied the issue, concluded just that. That organization was a defendant in the following case, *Kamakahi v. ASRM*, with respect to its attempt to promulgate guidelines for egg donations.[20]

## 4. CASE STUDY: KAMAKAHI V. AMERICAN SOCIETY FOR REPRODUCTIVE MEDICINE[21]

In this case, Lindsay Kamakahi brought a suit for herself and other similarly situated egg donors against ASRM and its affiliate, the Society for Assisted Reproductive Technology (SART).[22]

ASRM describes itself on its own website as an organization "dedicated to the advancement of the science and practice of reproductive medicine."[23] ASRM's affiliated organization, SART, describes itself as "the primary organization of professionals dedicated to the practice of assisted reproductive

---

[20] *Kamakahi*, 305 F.R.D. at 170.

[21] *Id.* at 164.

[22] *Id.* at 170.

[23] *ASRM's Mission, Vision, and Values*, REPRODUCTIVE FACTS, https://www.reproductivefacts.org/about-asrm/mission-statement/ (last visited June 17, 2023).

technologies (ART) in the United States."[24] The clinics that are a part of SART agree to be bound by any suggested ethical norms promulgated by ASRM.[25]

In 2000 and again in 2007, the Ethics Committee of ASRM had issued ethical guidelines including suggested compensation that should be paid to egg donors.[26] Specifically, any compensation for an egg donation above $5,000 would require special justification, and any amount above $10,000 was simply not appropriate.[27]

One legal scholar opined that the Ethics Committee suggested limiting compensation in order to preempt state regulation that might further restrict or even prohibit egg donations for compensation.[28] Nonetheless, the payment guidelines did represent a restriction on what egg donors might earn as compensation for their donation.

In accordance with their commitment to ASRM, SART clinics throughout the United States put those compensation guidelines into effect. Kamakahi, an

---

24 SOC'Y FOR ASSISTED REPROD. TECH., https://www.sart.org (last visited June 17, 2023).

25 *Kamakahi*, 305 F.R.D. at 171.

26 *Id.*

27 *Id.*

28 Miller, *supra* note 1, at 56 (citing Kim Krawiec, *Politics and Profits in the Egg Business (When Sunny Samaritans Sue, IV)*, FAC. LOUNGE (April 21, 2011, 7:12 PM), http://www.thefacultylounge.org/2011/04/politics-and-profits-in-the-egg-business-when-sunny-samaritans-sue-iv.html).

egg donor subjected to those compensation limits, alleged that the guidelines amounted to price fixing in violation of United States anti-trust laws.[29] Essentially, Kamakahi alleged that the suggested guidelines were anti-free market and limited her freedom to contract for whatever price the market would pay for her eggs.

Interestingly, the Ethics Committee had been evaluating whether egg donations for compensation demeaned or commodified women or the eggs that were effectively being sold.[30] In fact, the Ethics Committee concluded the opposite, that not paying women, or not allowing women the freedom to choose to participate in this market, was actually overly paternalistic and was in itself demeaning.[31] A prohibition would necessarily be based on the assumption that women are unable to effectively manage their own financial and reproductive lives.

The court never did render a final decision in the matter. Instead, after four years of litigation, the parties settled and ASRM agreed to rescind its ethical pricing guidelines.[32]

The *Kamakahi* case may well represent the state of the debate about the market for egg donations and surrogacy. With new forms of assisted reproductive technology coming into use by the 1980s, many voices expressed concern for the well-being of the women

---

[29] *Id.* at 34–35.

[30] *Id.* at 33.

[31] *Id.* at 34.

[32] *Id.* at 56.

who might be exploited through egg donations and surrogacy. *Kamakahi* suggests that the prevailing view in the United States more recently acknowledges and respects women's autonomy to make up their own minds about their reproductive capabilities and how to use them.

The concerns about exploitation, however, should be kept in mind so that safeguards continue to be put in place to assure that women who choose to be egg donors or surrogates are making free and informed decisions. One of the most important among those safeguards is the right of the egg donor or surrogate to her own attorney advisor.

## 5. NAVIGATING THE LAW

Legally, the egg donor should be allowed to hire her own attorney to represent her best interests in negotiating and executing an egg donor agreement with the intended parent(s). In many states, surrogacy statutes require that the surrogate be represented by an independent attorney. But with very little regulation in place regarding egg donations, there is not typically a requirement that the egg donor have an attorney. Regardless, egg donors should insist upon it. Moreover, the intended parents should pay the attorney's fees as part of the costs of the egg donor arrangement. If an agency is involved, the agency will usually insist upon this.

The egg donor should work with her attorney to understand any regulatory concerns relating to her donation. In most cases, this won't be much of an issue as egg donations are not regulated by most states in the United States.[33]

There are, however, some states that do categorically prohibit egg donations for compensation. Those states currently include: Georgia and Louisiana.[34] Egg donations should not be attempted in those states.

Some states have statutory safeguards in place for egg donors. In California, for example, any agency soliciting egg donations must post disclosures detailing the egg donation process and explaining that any egg donor must give her informed consent.[35] Arizona mandates that egg donors are treated like patients and receive due care from professionals.[36]

With reproductive laws relating to abortion currently in such flux in the United States, regulations relating to other aspects of women's reproductive freedom may also be in flux. So, it is crucial for the egg donor to work with her attorney to understand any current regulations that apply to her situation.

The egg donor also needs to work with her attorney to fully understand her commitments in the egg donor agreement, the associated risks, and negotiate

---

[33] Kitty L. Cone, *Eggs for Sale: The Scrambled State of Legislation in the Human Egg Market*, 35 UALR L. REV. 189, 190 (2012).

[34] GA. CODE ANN. § 16–12–160(a) (West 2023); LA STAT. ANN. § 9:122 (2023).

[35] CAL. HEALTH & SAFETY CODE § 125325 (West 2023).

[36] ARIZ. REV. STAT. ANN. § 36–1702(A) (2023).

for an arrangement that is acceptable to her. If there is anything about the agreement or the arrangement that the egg donor does not understand, she should ask her attorney for clarification. It is the attorney's responsibility to protect the best interests of his client.

**Egg Donors Need Independent Counsel**

One of the primary criticisms of both egg donation and surrogacy is the possibility that the women involved will be exploited. One important safeguard against this possibility is having the egg donor and surrogate each represented in their negotiations with intended parent(s) by their own independent attorneys. Happily for the egg donor and surrogate, their attorney's fees should be paid for by the intended parents.

As I always remind my own law students another word for attorney is counselor. In this case, an egg donor or surrogate's counsel should counsel their client so that the client fully understands the arrangement she would be undertaking, including all the related physical and psychological risks.

As with so many agreements, sometimes the best decision is a decision not to move forward. If the egg donor is uncomfortable for any reason, even if she just doesn't like the feeling she gets from the intended parents in negotiating the agreement, then she should consider ending the arrangement before becoming committed.

If, however, the egg donor has worked with her attorney and does feel comfortable that she fully understands the arrangement and is willing to take the associated risks, then the egg donor should move full steam ahead. As it has been for so many others who have been egg donors, like the super donor described at the beginning of this chapter, helping others with their family formation can be incredibly rewarding and fulfilling.

# CHAPTER 9

# THE EGG DONOR AGREEMENT

Like the surrogacy agreement, the egg donor agreement will follow a basic format, including prefatory clauses, representations, and commitments from the parties related to the various stages of egg donation, and boilerplate provisions.

The same basic contracting principles that applied to surrogacy contracts apply to egg donor contracts. This means that the drafters should draft the provisions in clear, plain English and avoid any unnecessarily complex sentences or legalese. And, of course, the top three rules to understanding a contract still apply:

(i) read the contract,

(ii) read the contract, and

(iii) read the $%#@ contract!

Thinking through, discussing, and agreeing on each issue helps ensure that the parties keep their promises, makes problems less likely, and makes formal dispute resolution unnecessary. This chapter will present samples of the key types of provisions you will need in an Egg Donor Agreement.

## 1. PREFATORY CLAUSES

The prefatory paragraphs, as mentioned with respect to the surrogacy agreement, set the stage for the agreements to come and create a tone for the relationship between the parties. Like surrogates, egg donors are generally compensated for their contribution.

Just as with surrogates, however many women become egg donors out of a desire to help others. Egg donors themselves may have been born through a type of assisted reproductive technology or have some other personal reason for wanting to help in this regard. The spirit of this generosity can be captured in the prefatory clauses, which in many ways mirror those in the surrogacy agreement. The provisions below show sample prefatory clauses.

**Prefatory Clauses**

**Where:** the Intended Parents are unable to have genetically related children of their own and seek to work with the Egg Donor to have one or more genetically related children; and

**Where:** the Egg Donor is sympathetic to the needs of the Intended Parents, and seeks to help the Intended Parents have one or more children by embarking on the egg-donation arrangement described here; and

**Where:** as a result, the Intended Parents are incredibly appreciative of Egg Donor's willingness to help and commit to compensate her as outlined in this agreement; and

**Where:** the parties understand that all the medical procedures associated with this egg donation arrangement, including hyper-stimulation of the ovaries and egg retrieval are inherently risky; and

| |
|---|
| **Where:** despite those risks, the parties to this agreement herein set forth with specificity their mutual intention that the Egg Donor: (i) take medication to hyper-stimulate her ovaries, (ii) submit to a procedure to retrieve her eggs; and (iii) donate those eggs to the Intended Parents for their use as described herein; and |
| **Where:** the Intended Parents will take full parental responsibility for, and custody of, any children born with the donated eggs; and the Egg Donor [and her partner or spouse] waive any parental rights that they otherwise may have to the children so born; |
| Now therefore, the parties agree. . . |

## 2. DEFINITIONS

Readers should pay careful attention to the definition section of an egg donor agreement because, as with surrogacy agreements, rights and obligations are often determined through those defined terms.

| **Definitions** |
|---|
| **Permitted Use**—the Intended Parents shall have the right to fertilize the donated eggs and transfer one or more of the resulting embryos into a gestational surrogate in hopes of having one or more children; they may also freeze any resulting embryos, donate them [at no cost] to another person or couple to use them to become parents, donate them [at no cost] for scientific research, or allow them to be destroyed. |

Notice with this definition that the parties specified what the donated eggs can be used for. This is one of the major issues confronting egg donors and intended parents. Egg donors may only want their eggs to be used by the particular intended parent or parents who they are familiar with through their agency. The egg donor may not know the identity of the intended parents, but she would likely want to have a general understanding about who the intended parents are. For example, the egg donor may want to know whether the intended parents are financially stable, well educated, and able to provide for any children who are produced out of the agreement. The egg donor therefore may not agree to allow the intended parents to donate her eggs.

There is a market for unused frozen embryos where intended parents with excess frozen embryos sell them to subsequent intended parents as a way to hedge the costs associated with surrogacy.[1] As with surrogacy, each state can regulate the transfer of embryos with its own law. Some states, like Florida, Louisiana, and Oklahoma specifically make the sale of embryos illegal.[2] Accordingly, if intended parents do want to sell their embryos they will need to proceed with caution, and understand the law in the state where they will proceed. As always, it is best to

---

[1] *See* I. Glenn Cohen & Eli Y. Adashi, *Made-to-Order Embryos for Sale—A Brave New World?*, 368 NEW ENG. J. MED. 2517 (2013) (examining the risks associated with the sale of "made-to-order embryos").

[2] FLA. STAT. ANN. § 873.05(1) (West 2023); LA. STAT. ANN. § 9:122 (2023); OKLA. STAT. ANN. tit. 10, § 556(E)(2) (West 2023).

get advice from your attorney who specializes in reproductive law.

Note that selling embryos is not a *Permitted Use* in the sample definition above. In that definition, only subsequent donations of unused embryos were allowed, but not sales of unused embryos. If the donor does not care, then the intended parents may indeed want the ability to recoup some of their expenses by selling any resulting unused embryos. Here, as always, it is important for the parties to pay careful attention to the definitions because they may address major rights and obligations of the parties.

## 3. REPRESENTATIONS

Both the intended parents and the egg donor will want certain assurances from their counterparty before entering into the transaction. These representations are quite analogous to the representations that the parties make in a surrogacy agreement. For example, both parties will want to know whether the other party fully understands their commitments and the risks associated with the process. The parties may insist that each party has undergone mental health and legal counseling in connection with the egg donation.

### A. REPRESENTATIONS OF EGG DONOR

One important representation that the intended parents should consider is whether the egg donor has been a successful donor previously. Success is measured by a previous egg donation resulting in childbirth. One of the primary reasons intended parents may choose a particular donor is because she has a successful history of donating.

The other reason why intended parents may choose one egg donor over another is related to her profile. Generally, egg donors fill out profiles by supplying information about themselves including their physical attributes, talents, hobbies, their own medical history, and information about their family medical history. Profiles generally include a variety of pictures of the donor at different ages and possibly members of her family, including any children she has had.

Intended parents will want assurances that the information in the profile is accurate and not misleading. Agencies and IVF clinics that find donors for intended parents generally try to verify the information supplied, but a representation in the egg donor agreement can supplement any agency or clinic's effort to verify that information.

**Representations of the Egg Donor**

The Intended Parents will want the egg donor to attest to a variety of facts. Some of these may include:

- that she is of a certain age (over twenty-one but under thirty-one);[3]

[3] Our IVF clinic recommended that egg donors be older than twenty-one years old, but younger than thirty or thirty-one in order to donate the most viable eggs.

- that she is either single or part of a couple, married or otherwise (if part of a couple, the partner or spouse will generally be required to sign on to the agreement);
- that she is competent to execute the agreement and fully understands the nature of the egg donor arrangement;
- that she is healthy and, at least to the best of her knowledge, can successfully undergo the egg donation procedures;
- [if true] that she has been a successful egg donor previously in that [out of x donations y] donations have resulted in a live birth;
- that the information in her Donor Profile is accurate and not misleading in any way;
- that she fully understands the risks, both medical and psychological, associated with being an egg donor, including possible infections, and, in the extreme, complications that could even be fatal;
- that she has received mental health counseling about the obligations and risks associated with egg donations; and
- that she has received legal counseling about her risks, rights, and obligations as they pertain to egg donation generally, and also as they are described in this Egg Donor Agreement.

## B. REPRESENTATIONS OF THE INTENDED PARENTS

Similarly, the egg donor will want to know that they are working with intended parents who are competent enough to enter into the arrangement and who understand all the risks, including the fact that egg donations do not always result in live births even after appropriate fertilization and implantation into a gestational surrogate. The egg donor will want to ensure that the intended parents understand that the egg donor's responsibilities are limited to her donation. The box below contains some sample representations of the intended parents.

**Representations of the Intended Parents**

The egg donor will want the Intended Parents to attest to a variety of facts. Some of these may include:

- that the intended parent is either a single person or part of a couple, married or otherwise (if part of a couple, the partner or spouse will generally be required to sign on to the agreement);
- that they are competent to execute the agreement and fully understand the nature of the egg donor arrangement;
- that they fully understand the risks, both medical and psychological, associated with egg donation, including the fact that a wide range in the number of eggs retrieved is possible, and that an IVF procedure with

donor eggs is not always successful, nor does every pregnancy result in a live birth, due to no fault of the egg donor;

- that they have received mental health counseling about the obligations and risks associated with egg donation; and
- that they have received legal counseling about their risks, rights, and obligations as they pertain to the egg donation generally, and also as they are described in this Egg Donor Agreement.

## 4. MEDICAL TESTING AND AGREEMENT TO SHARE INFORMATION

As with the surrogate, the intended parents and the responsible physicians will likely want to run a number of medical tests on the egg donor. In particular, the physician will screen the egg donor to determine whether she is a carrier of any genetic diseases that may be passed on to a child born from her eggs. The physician will also screen the egg donor to assure that she is physically capable of undergoing the egg donation procedures.

The egg donor will be asked to share the results of the tests with the intended parents. The intended parents have a right to terminate the arrangement if the results indicate any risk from proceeding with that egg donor. Some sample clauses regarding testing of an egg donor are listed below.

**Testing of Egg Donor**

**Egg Donor's Agreement to Submit to Testing.** The Egg Donor agrees to submit to any and all medical, psychological, and genetic testing deemed prudent or required by any Responsible Physician.

**Agreement to Share Information.** The Egg Donor agrees to provide the Intended Parents and all Responsible Physicians with access to the results of all relevant medical, mental health, and genetic tests and to execute any additional documents necessary to assure that access.

**Termination Upon Unsatisfactory Results.** If any of the results of the medical, mental health, or genetic testing is unsatisfactory to the Intended Parents, this agreement will terminate and the Intended Parents will have no further obligations due or owing hereunder.

## 5. MEDICAL PROCEDURES, BEHAVIOR RESTRICTIONS, AND ASSUMPTION OF RISK

Once the preliminary testing is done, the medical procedures begin. These include hyper-stimulation of the ovaries to produce multiple eggs, sometimes as many as twenty, and egg retrieval.

In accord with the earlier representation, the egg donor must affirmatively acknowledge that she understands all the related risks and still agrees to undergo the procedures. Sample clauses regarding an egg donor's submission to the medical procedures are listed below.

| **Submission to Medical Procedures** |
|---|
| **Medical Procedures.** The Egg Donor agrees to undergo all the procedures related to the Egg Donation, including taking medication to hyper-stimulate her ovaries and then have the resulting eggs retrieved through a surgical procedure. The Egg Donor further agrees to cooperate fully with any Responsible Physician to assure that these procedures have the highest chance of success.<br>**Assumed Risks.** The Egg Donor [and her partner/spouse] acknowledge[s] that she [they] understand[s] the medical and psychological risks associated with these procedures, including in the extreme, the possibility of the Egg Donor's death due to complications, and agree[s] not to hold the Intended Parents responsible for any of those risks. |

As with the surrogate, the egg donor must also agree to follow any behavioral restrictions advised by a responsible physician in connection with the egg donation. For example, the hyper-stimulation of the egg donor's ovaries creates additional risks of natural pregnancy through sexual intercourse. A responsible physician is likely to advise the egg donor to use particular forms of contraception during the process or avoid sexual intercourse completely. A sample clause that outlines potential behavioral restrictions is listed below.

**Behavioral Restrictions**

**Behavioral Restrictions.** The Egg Donor also agrees to follow the behavioral guidelines of any Responsible Physician in order to assure the highest degree of success with the procedures. This includes taking any medication as it is prescribed, attending appointments, allowing testing and blood draws. It also may include refraining from sexual intercourse for a certain amount of time before the Egg Donation or using a particular kind of contraception. Any violation of this provision will be deemed a material breach of the agreement by the Egg Donor and will allow the Intended Parents the option to terminate their obligations hereunder. Any child the Egg Donor may conceive due to hyper-stimulation of her ovaries will be the child of the Egg Donor and the Intended Parents will have no parental responsibility for such child.

## 6. PARENTAL RIGHTS AND OBLIGATIONS

Central to the surrogacy arrangement is the agreement between the parties that any child born from the donated eggs will be the child of the intended parents and not the egg donor or the egg donor's partner or spouse.

Thus, there are two sets of commitments that must be made: the intended parents' commitment to take full parental responsibility and custody of any children born from the donated eggs, and the egg donor and her partner or spouse's commitment not to assert any such parental rights. The box below lists sample clauses regarding the parental responsibility for any child born as a result of the egg donation process.

| Parental Responsibility for Any Child Born |
|---|
| **Intended Parents Commit to Full Parental Responsibility.** The Intended Parents commit to take full parental responsibility for and custody of any child born from the donated eggs immediately upon the birth of such child. This commitment shall be unwavering, regardless of any medical condition or affliction that may affect any such child.<br><br>**Egg Donor Waives Any Parental Rights.** Egg Donor [and her partner or spouse] agree[s] to waive any parental rights they may have with respect to any children born from the egg donation and not to assert any claim to parental rights or custody. Egg Donor [and her partner or spouse] also agrees to cooperate to the fullest extent to support and enforce the parental rights of the Intended Parents, including cooperating in any necessary legal proceedings. |

## 7. PERMITTED USES

Defining the permitted uses for the donated eggs and any resulting embryos is not sufficient alone to create a binding commitment between the parties. Thus, there must be a specific section addressing the permitted uses. This section will likely follow the section explaining parental rights. The language need not use specifically defined terms, but it must identify what the egg donor is willing to accept as the permitted uses for her donation.

The possibilities include the following: the fertilization and then implantation of the resulting embryo into a gestational surrogate in an attempt to have a resulting child or children; the cryopreservation of any resulting embryos not used immediately upon their creation; the donation [at no cost] for scientific research or donation [at no cost] to another potential intended parent; the sale to another intended parent; or destruction of the resulting embryos. Some form agreements include all of the above options and require the parties to initial the acceptable choices. A negotiated agreement, on the other hand, will state affirmatively what options are permitted by the egg donor as a condition of her donation. Refer back earlier in this chapter to the definition of Permitted Uses for an example of these types of options. The drafter can use this kind of defined term, if desired, but the affirmative commitment is still essential.

| Permitted Uses |
| --- |
| **Permitted Uses.** The parties agree that the Intended Parents may use the donated eggs for any Permitted Use. |

## 8. FINANCIAL ISSUES

The financial issues involved with egg donations tend to be more straightforward than in surrogacy arrangements. The intended parents will generally agree to a specific base compensation for the egg donor, but then also agree to pay or reimburse for medical and any other expenses that the egg donor incurs that are related to the donation. All the parties will want to pay close attention to the commitments here and make sure that the financial arrangements are acceptable for all.

## A. BASE COMPENSATION

Generally, the intended parents pay the fee up front either directly to the egg donor or through an agency or IVF clinic. Payments through agencies or clinics include any additional fee charged by the agency or clinic. Base fees for egg donations vary considerably, but most range between $5,000 and $15,000. Agency fees or clinic fees would be in addition to that amount and can double this amount.

| **Fees** |
|---|
| **Base Compensation.** The Intended Parents agree to pay the Egg Donor for her services base compensation of [$10,000]. [This amount is payable to the Agency or IVF Clinic and should be paid together with the Agency Fee or the IVF Clinic Fee.]<br><br>**Timing of Base Compensation.** The Base Compensation is due upon execution of this Egg Donor Agreement. |

## B. EXPENSE AND REIMBURSEMENT PAYMENTS

The intended parents generally also make financial commitments to pay for any and all medical costs and any other out-of-pocket expenses that the egg donor may have, including legal fees. It is also not uncommon for intended parents to find an egg donor who does not live in the state where the IVF clinic is located. Thus, the intended parents typically pay for or reimburse the egg donor for travel expenses for the donor and a companion. The egg donor may also ask the intended parents to pay for medical costs related to any complication caused as a direct result of the egg donation. These expenses and reimbursements can significantly increase the overall costs of egg donation.

| Expenses and Reimbursements |
| --- |
| **Expense and Reimbursement Payments.** The Intended Parents also agree to pay directly, if possible, or else to reimburse Egg Donor for, any and all out-of-pocket expenses related to the Egg Donation that are not covered by any applicable insurance. These expenses include, but are not limited to, expenses related to the egg donation for:<br>• Medical testing;<br>• Mental health counseling;<br>• Medical procedures;<br>• Any medications or vitamins recommended or required by any Responsible Physician; |

- Medical fees for any complications that are directly caused by the Egg Donation;
- Reasonable legal fees payable to her attorney;
- [if egg donor has any children] any childcare required by Egg Donor to facilitate her service and attendance at appointments, not to exceed a total of [$200];
- [if Egg Donor will travel from another city] any reasonable travel expenses for Egg Donor and one companion, including coach airfare if Egg Donor will fly to accommodate the Intended Parents' choice of IVF Clinic, two nights at a [three-star] hotel or better, and a [$100] per diem for miscellaneous expenses and meals.

Timing of Expense and Reimbursement Payments. Any such expense or reimbursement payment is due at the time when it is incurred.

## 9. MISCELLANEOUS PROVISIONS

Just as with the surrogacy agreement, certain provisions are often included at the end under a "Miscellaneous" category. These provisions are also sometimes referred to as boilerplate. But do not let the fact that these provisions are referred to as miscellaneous or boilerplate lead you to overlook them. Read and understand these provisions just as you do every other provision of the agreement.

## A. CHOICE-OF-LAW

For example, the miscellaneous provisions often include provisions on the governing law and any agreement on a venue for dispute resolution. The choice-of-law and venue provisions will likely reflect the same law and venue chosen for the surrogacy agreement, but parties should seek advice of counsel for this decision.

| Choice of Law and Venue |
| --- |
| **Choice of Law and Venue.** The parties hereto agree that this agreement, its validity, interpretation, and performance and any other disputes hereunder will be subject to the laws of [Illinois]. The parties also agree to submit their dispute to the [courts of Illinois]. |

## B. CONFIDENTIALITY

Confidentiality may also be addressed in the miscellaneous section of agreement. Egg donors can be anonymous, as often happens, or they can be open donors. For an anonymous egg donation, the intended parents review the profile of the egg donor, but never learn her name or her contact information. With an open donor, the intended parents learn the donor's name and are in direct communication with her. An open donor arrangement is typically the case when the egg donor is either a friend or family of the intended parents. Normally, agencies and clinics help intended parents find egg donors, but the donor remains anonymous. This approach requires the parties to make certain commitments regarding the confidentiality of the process.

When considering confidentiality, it is also important to recognize that in certain circumstances medical necessities might warrant the resulting child knowing who their egg donor was. For example, the parties need to consider when it would be helpful for the child to be able to contact the egg donor to obtain information about her family's medical background or request a blood, organ, or tissue donation from the egg donor or someone in the egg donor's family. In the egg donor agreement, the egg donor may agree to be contacted in that event.

Further, any child born from an egg donation may simply want to meet their egg donor at some point. The parties may agree on what happens in this circumstance, like perhaps allowing the child to meet the donor when the child reaches a predetermined age. The sample language set forth below addresses the possibility of contact for medical purposes or for a method to meet if agreed upon by all parties.

| Confidentiality |
| --- |
| **Confidentiality.** The parties agree to proceed with the Egg Donation anonymously and not to seek out the identity of their counterparties. If any of the parties inadvertently learn the identity of a counterparty, they agree to keep such identity confidential. |

Intended Parents agree to destroy any information they received in connection with the egg donation relating to the identity of the egg donor.

Notwithstanding the foregoing, if any Child born as a result of the Egg Donation has a medical need to contact the Egg Donor, then the Intended Parents or such Child may attempt such contact through [the Agency or the IVF Clinic]. In such case, [the Agency or the IVF Clinic] will contact Egg Donor who shall cooperate to allow the contact.

If any Child born as a result of the Egg Donation is simply curious to meet Egg Donor, then after such Child's [18th] birthday, such Child can request that the Agency or the IVF Clinic contact Egg Donor and make a request for contact. Egg Donor will have sole discretion in that case to decide whether to proceed with such contact.

Egg Donor [and her partner or spouse] agree[s] not to initiate any contact with the Intended Parents or with any child born from the egg donation under any circumstances.

The egg donor agreement is a roadmap of what to expect from the egg donation process and what commitments each of the parties makes in connection with that process. The parties should read through the agreement thoroughly, discuss it with their attorneys, make sure they understand each provision, and negotiate for any changes that they think are appropriate.

This process should lead to an arrangement that all of the parties accept, minimizing the likelihood of any problems along the way, and making any formal dispute resolution unlikely. While not all egg donations result in a live birth for the intended parents, if it is successful, the egg donor will have helped the intended parents achieve their dream of having children.

# CHAPTER 10

# FUNDAMENTAL AND EQUAL RIGHTS

Beyond the contract law issues, surrogacy also implicates profound constitutional issues. The ability of any individual (and by association any couple) to have natural children and raise them the way they see fit has repeatedly been said by United States federal courts to be a fundamental constitutional right. Going back 100 years, the U.S. Supreme Court held that parents have a liberty interest under the 5th and 14th Amendments of the Constitution "to marry, establish a home, and bring up children."[1]

## 1. RECENT CASES

A fundamental constitutional right for a woman to choose to have an abortion at certain times during her pregnancy had been established in *Roe v. Wade* and then further nuanced in *Planned Parenthood v. Casey*.[2] Those cases were overturned by *Dobbs v. Jackson Women's Health Organization* in 2022.[3] Perhaps more specifically relevant for surrogacy, in the aftermath of *Dobbs*, the Alabama Supreme Court in *LePage v Center for Reproductive Medicine* ruled that embryos created through IVF are "unborn

---

1 Meyer v. Nebraska, 262 U.S. 390, 399 (1923). That case involved a prohibition on teaching German to school children.

2 Roe v. Wade, 410 U.S. 113 (1973); Planned Parenthood v. Casey, 505 U.S. 833 (1992).

3 Dobbs v. Jackson Women's Health Organization, 597 U.S. 215 (2022).

children."[4] Thus, the state's wrongful death statute could be applied when and if embryos are accidentally destroyed.[5] An implication of the case is also that the intentional destruction of an embryo could well amount to murder. While the state did pass a statute quickly immunizing IVF clinics from both civil and criminal liability for the accidental destruction of embryos, pressure on IVF remains.[6] Since IVF is central to a surrogacy arrangement, if IVF is limited or curtailed in certain states, surrogacy most certainly will be also.

At the same time constitutional law is implicated in an equal rights context. In our situation, we found that the federal government, which had allowed tax deductions for medical expenses related to surrogacy, did not allow those deductions for us.

The federal Internal Revenue Service (IRS) decided that because we were not technically infertile, but merely two gay men deciding to have a family, we didn't have a medical necessity that needed treatment. Thus, they decided, we could not deduct our significant expenses. A heterosexual couple, by contrast, would typically be pursuing surrogacy specifically because of a fertility issue. So, that opposite sex couple would have a medical necessity for pursuing surrogacy. We actually challenged the IRS decision and brought suit in federal court, taking it up to the federal court of

---

[4] LePage v. Center for Reproductive Medicine, P.C. No. SC–2022–0515 (Sup. Ct. Al, 2024)

[5] *Id.*

[6] ALA. CODE § 6–5–811 (2024).

appeals for the 11th Circuit (of which Florida is a part).

Unfortunately, in front of the conservative federal courts in the Southeast, we lost. A telling portion in the opinion from the 11th Circuit gives some insights into the discriminatory bias we felt underscored the decision. In their discussion of reproduction, the court, apparently in an attempt at humor, tells its readers that it was necessary in our case to educate (the public, presumably) "with a primer on the science of human reproduction."[7] Through this discussion, the court explains that reproduction takes a male and a female.[8] Perhaps the judge writing the opinion really felt it necessary to educate the public on this point. Or, more likely, it seems the 11th Circuit panel was uncomfortable with the notion of two men having a child together, but comfortable enough to lampoon the idea for posterity in their opinion.

We still believe strongly that our treatment was discriminatory, unreasonable, and unconstitutional. I would have liked to take our case up to the Supreme Court, but was advised by civil rights advocates that with the composition of the Supreme Court, by then majority conservative, we might only give the Court an opportunity to set equal rights back.

Our case illustrates the intersection of the fundamental constitutional right to form a family

---

[7] Morrissey v. United States, 871 F.3d 1260, 1266 (11th Cir. 2017).

[8] *Id.*

with the equal protection argument that the government should not discriminate without a constitutionally acceptable reason. We still see no reason at all for the discrimination in our case.

## 2. FUNDAMENTAL RIGHTS

Fundamental rights spring from the Fifth and Fourteenth Amendments to the United States Constitution. Both the Fifth and the Fourteenth Amendments to the United States Constitution contain a Due Process Clause. Pursuant to the Fifth Amendment, the federal government cannot deprive an individual of "life, liberty, or property, without due process of law."[9] The Fourteenth Amendment contains the same language but applies to state governments.[10] The Due Process Clause has both a procedural and a substantive component.

Procedurally, the government can't deprive an individual of a protected life, liberty, or property interest without providing sufficient procedural safeguards. Procedural safeguards include hearings before impartial decision makers to determine if, in the given case, the government has a constitutionally sufficient reason for impinging on the life, liberty, or property interests of the individual.

Substantive due process, by contrast, means that the life, liberty, and property described in the Due Process Clause include a wide array of substantive rights that the government should not infringe

---

[9] U.S. CONST. amend. V.

[10] U.S. CONST. amend. XIV, § 1.

without a constitutionally sufficient justification. The federal courts have developed a system for categorizing those rights. Some are deemed fundamental while others are not.

If a right is not deemed fundamental, then the government action only needs to meet a low, so-called rational basis, level of scrutiny. The government action need only be rationally related to any legitimate government goal for the government action to be upheld.[11] The Supreme Court has held, for example, that economic rights are not fundamental.[12] Thus, economic restrictions imposed by the government only need to be rationally related to a legitimate government interest.

Fundamental rights, however, require that the government meet a very high degree of strict scrutiny before being allowed to impinge on that right. The language the courts uses in those cases is that the government action must be necessary to achieve a compelling goal in order for the government to be allowed to impinge on a fundamental right.[13]

| Substantive Due Process |
| --- |
| **Fundamental Right → Strict Scrutiny,** the action must be necessary to achieve a compelling goal |

[11] *See* Williamson v. Lee Optical, Inc., 348 U.S. 483, 491 (1955).

[12] *Id.*

[13] Loving v. Virginia, 388 U.S. 1, 11 (1967).

**Non-fundamental Right → Rational Basis,** the action must be rationally related to a legitimate purpose

In practice, it has been very difficult for the state to meet the strict scrutiny test and justify imposing on fundamental rights once those rights have been found to exist. By contrast, it is relatively easy for the state to meet the rational basis test.

The Supreme Court of the United States repeatedly has said that the liberty interest of the Due Process Clause includes fundamental rights related to family formation. In a landmark case from the 1940s, the Supreme Court stated that the right to have children is "one of the basic civil rights of man."[14] Later, in the 1970s, the Supreme Court announced that "[i]f the right of privacy means anything, it is the right of the individual, married or single, to be free from unwarranted government intrusion into matters so fundamentally affecting a person as the decision whether to bear or beget a child."[15]

## 3. EQUAL PROTECTION

Equal protection also springs specifically from the Fourteenth Amendment to the U.S. Constitution, which states that "nor shall any State . . . deny to any person . . . *the equal protection of the laws* without

[14] Skinner v. Oklahoma *ex rel.* Williamson, 316 U.S. 535, 541 (1942).

[15] Eisenstadt v. Baird, 405 U.S. 438, 453 (1972).

due process."[16] That Equal Protection Clause has been held to be implicit in the Fifth Amendment, even though it is not explicitly stated there. Thus, neither the federal (under the Fifth Amendment), nor any state government (under the Fourteenth Amendment) can deprive any individual of the equal protection of the law.

Equal protection jurisprudence involves first identifying the group being discriminated against. If certain suspect categories, like those based on race or religion, are used by the government, then the action needs to be justified by applying strict scrutiny. So, the government action has to be necessary to achieve a compelling government interest.[17]

If the category is based on other traits, for example, socio-economic status, then the government action can be justified by using the lowest level of judicial scrutiny, rational basis.[18] Government action in those cases need only to be rationally related to a legitimate governmental goal. Equal protection jurisprudence has evolved to include an intermediate category of scrutiny for regulations based on sex and regulations that affect children born to single parents. In those cases, regulations need to be substantially related to achieving important government goals.[19]

---

[16] U.S. CONST. amend. XIV, § 1 (emphasis added).

[17] Strict scrutiny was first applied in an equal protection analysis in Korematsu v. United States, 323 U.S. 214, 216 (1944).

[18] Maher v. Roe, 432 U.S. 464, 471 (1977).

[19] United States v. Virginia, 518 U.S. 515, 555 (1996).

| **Equal Protection** |
|---|
| **Is class based on race or nationality → Strict Scrutiny,** the action must be necessary to achieve a compelling goal; |
| **Is class based on sex or children born to a single parent → Intermediate Scrutiny,** the action must be furthering an important purpose; |
| **Any other class → Rational Basis,** the action must be rationally related to a legitimate purpose. |

One of the most famous cases involving family formation is *Loving v. Virginia* from 1967.[20] The *Loving* case involved the right of an interracial couple to begin their family by getting married.[21]

Virginia, where the couple was living, had made mixed race marriages illegal and the couple challenged that law. Virginia wasn't alone. At the time, 16 states had these so-called anti-miscegenation laws, laws which criminalized interracial marriage.[22]

Using both a fundamental rights analysis *and* an equal protection analysis, the Supreme Court struck down the law.[23] The Supreme Court found that marriage was a fundamental right under the substantive Due Process Clause of the

---

20 Loving v. Virginia, 388 U.S. 1 (1967).

21 *Id.* at 12.

22 *Id.* at 6.

23 *Id.* at 8–12.

Constitution.[24] Further, the government did not have a sufficient justification for violating that fundamental right.[25] The Court went on to say that the equal protection analysis required the government to treat all citizens the same, regardless of race.[26] The Court found that the statute was based on discrimination which violated the Equal Protection Clause of the Constitution.[27]

## 4. FROM THE FERTILITY CLINIC TO THE 11TH CIRCUIT COURT[28]

As a same-sex couple, building our family through surrogacy was not only challenging, but also quite expensive. We knew that the tax code in the United States allowed tax deductions for medical expenses related to any function of the body.[29] We added up our own expenses and took the deductions as expenses related to our reproductive function. Unfortunately, the IRS did not agree with our position. After an investigation, our deductions were denied.[30]

---

24 *Id.* at 12.

25 *Id.*

26 *Id.* at 11–12.

27 *Id.* at 12.

28 See Joseph F. Morrissey, *Rejecting Instrumentalism: Medical Deductions for Family Formation Denied*, 23 J. GENDER, RACE & JUST. 365 (2021), for a full discussion of our case against the IRS. Parts of that article have been reprinted and included here.

29 I.R.C. § 213.

30 Letter from Malcolm T. Haile, Sr., Supervisory Revenue Agent, I.R.S. to author (July 20, 2014) (on file with author).

By then, we were aware that the IRS had allowed for the deduction of medical expenses related to family formation for opposite-sex couples, dating all the way back to 1994.[31] We could not understand why we would be treated differently, especially after landmark Supreme Court cases like *United States v. Windsor* had already vindicated the rights of same-sex couples to be treated the same as opposite-sex couples under the United States tax code.[32]

The Supreme Court decided *United States v. Windsor* in 2013.[33] *Windsor* struck down the part of the federal Defense of Marriage Act (DOMA) that provided a marriage had to be between a man and a woman, paving the way for same-sex marriage to become legal throughout the United States.[34]

The issue in *Windsor* was whether a same-sex couple, residents of New York but married in Canada, would get the benefit of marriage protections in the taxation of one of the spouse's estate after she had died.[35] Typically, amounts left to a surviving spouse by the deceased spouse were entitled to an estate tax deduction. Since the couple

---

[31] *See generally* Sedgwick v. Comm'r, No. 10133-94 (T.C. filed June 14, 1994) (noting that the IRS settled with an opposite sex couple regarding their deduction for expenses related to IVF and surrogacy).

[32] *See* United States v. Windsor, 570 U.S. 744, 775 (2013) (determining that the Defense of Marriage Act violated the Fifth Amendment by providing that "marriage" was only a legal union between a man and a woman).

[33] United States v. Windsor, 570 U.S. 744, 749–52 (2013).

[34] *Id.* at 775.

[35] *Id.* at 750–51.

was recognized as being married under New York law, the surviving spouse, Edith Windsor, sued the federal government to be given the usual marital estate tax deduction. The federal government had initially denied the deduction because DOMA provided that the federal government would not recognize same-sex marriages.

In its opinion, the Court discussed both of the constitutional provisions highlighted above to reach their decision: the substantive due process liberty interest inherent in the Fifth Amendment *and* the Equal Protection Clause.[36] The Court ruled that the Due Process Clause of the Fifth Amendment meant that the surviving spouse could not be deprived of her status as a married person by DOMA, and that she was fully entitled to the tax benefits that any married person would get.[37] Moreover, under the Equal Protection Clause, the Supreme Court found that with DOMA the federal government was specifically targeting gay and lesbian people married under state law, and denying them the same rights that opposite-sex couples would enjoy.[38] Although the Supreme Court did not announce what level of scrutiny targeting gay people as a class would receive, the Court did find that the discriminatory treatment in that case was unconstitutional.[39]

At a time when gay rights were being vindicated throughout the United States and the world, it

---

[36] *Id.* at 769–75.

[37] *Id.* at 775.

[38] *Id.* at 769–70.

[39] *Id.* at 775.

seemed only right that we should invoke the medical deductions provision of the tax code and apply it to our own situation. If the Supreme Court thought Edith Windsor should get the same tax deductions as people in opposite-sex relationships, then surely the IRS should follow that precedent with us.

Those tax deductions can ultimately reduce the expenses of family formation and, for some, might even make the difference between deciding to have a family or not. For ourselves, but also for every other person not in a traditional marriage who wishes to pursue family formation and receive the tax benefits that flow from deducting the medical expenses, we sued.

The IRS official auditing our tax return had been unwavering in his conclusion. Our decision to build a family as two gay men was merely our "choice," he explained unabashedly, and all related expenses would not be subsidized by the United States government through the medical deduction provision.[40]

Our arguments to the federal courts circled around two points. First, that the statute did not demand any "but for" necessity for medical expenses to be deductible.[41] Instead, the statute merely stated that deductions were allowed for expenses related to any

---

[40] Telephone Conversation with Gary Shepherd, IRS Agent (June 2014).

[41] I.R.C. § 213.

function of the body.[42] Our expenses, of course, were related to the reproductive function.

Second, to the extent the statute was going to be applied to deny us the deduction, it treated us differently from people in opposite-sex relationships in violation of the Equal Protection Clause of the Fifth Amendment. Moreover, that differential treatment impacted our ability to effectively exercise a fundamental right—our right to have children.

In the Federal District Court in Tampa, Judge Richard Lazzara ruled on a motion for summary judgment that the expenses related to IVF and surrogacy were not expenses that were related to the taxpayer, his spouse, or a dependent.[43] This language mirrored the language used by the IRS in its letter denying the deduction.[44] Judge Lazzara simply did not agree that the expenses at stake were undertaken in connection with the reproductive function of the taxpayer's body.[45] Judge Lazzara further reasoned that any unmarried heterosexual male could and would be treated the same way under the statute were they to pursue IVF and surrogacy for any reason unrelated to an infertile spouse.[46]

---

42 *Id.*

43 Morrissey v. United States, 226 F. Supp. 3d 1338, 1341–42 (M.D. Fla. 2016).

44 Letter from Malcolm T. Haile, Sr., *supra* note 25.

45 *See Morrissey*, 226 F. Supp. 3d at 1343.

46 *Id.*

Thus, there was no constitutional infirmity in the denial of the deduction either.[47]

As *Windsor* pointed out, it is constitutionally impermissible to treat people in same-sex relationships differently than people in opposite-sex relationships without a constitutionally sufficient justification.[48] Because the IRS has allowed medical deductions in cases like mine where the couples involved were opposite-sex, we argued that the IRS's denial of the deduction in my case violated substantive due process and the Equal Protection Clause of the Fifth Amendment. Both of those provisions supported the Court's conclusion in *Windsor*, and both, we argued, supported the IRS granting me the medical expense deduction.[49]

Coupled with the IRS's different treatment of me in comparison to opposite-sex couples was a clear discriminatory animus on the part of the IRS. The Supreme Court specifically has ruled that animus against a politically unpopular group cannot sustain government action even under the rational basis test.[50] In our case the discriminatory animus by the government was shown when the IRS agent reviewing my deduction in the first instance explained that deciding not to have children sexually with a woman was simply my choice. Calling my being gay a choice reflects outmoded thinking which

---

[47] *Id.* at 1344–45.

[48] United States v. Windsor, 570 U.S. 744, 774 (2013).

[49] Opening Brief of Plaintiff-Appellant at 43–44, Morrissey v. United States, 871 F.3d 1260 (11th Cir. 2017) (No. 17-10685).

[50] Romer v. Evans, 517 U.S. 620, 631–36 (1996).

condemns gay people for making an immoral choice to be gay, one that the government should not support. That IRS agent's decision was confirmed by his manager and on appeal at the IRS, with both higher-level decision makers showing deference to his conclusion.

The district court dismissed our constitutional claim, primarily because it believed it already established that the government was merely applying the statute in an even-handed way, and therefore, in no way, was being discriminatory.[51] After all, according to the court, a single straight man would be treated the same way. Once again, this ignored the relevant facts, just discussed above, that lead to the opposite conclusion. The opposite-sex couples who could not have children without medical intervention have been granted the deduction for their related medical expenses, while we, in the context of a same-sex relationship, were not.

In the court's explanation of the constitutional dimensions of the case, the federal court opinion actually cites *Lofton v. Secretary of the Department of Children and Family Services*, a 2004 case that upheld Florida's blanket statutory prohibition on gay adoptions.[52] *Lofton* was never technically overturned, but was discredited when the state courts in Florida

---

51 *Morrissey*, 871 F.3d at 1271.

52 *Id.* at 1268 (citing Lofton v. Sec'y of the Dep't of Children & Family Servs., 358 F.3d 804, 818 (11th Cir. 2004)).

invalidated that statute, and the Florida legislature finally rescinded it.[53]

The federal court in our case did not need to cite to *Lofton,* but did so to explain that equal protection claims receive rational basis review when there is no fundamental right or suspect class implicated.[54] Given that the *Lofton* case has been discredited, the court's reliance on that case to buttress a basic point that is discussed in many cases is perhaps telling. That adoption ban itself was passed with legislative comments expressly saying to the gay community "[w]e're really tired of you. We wish you'd go back in the closet."[55] Once again, the Supreme Court specifically ruled that discriminatory animus against a politically unpopular group is an impermissible

[53] Lofton v. Sec'y of the Dep't of Children & Family Servs., 358 F.3d 804, 806 (11th Cir. 2004), *cert. denied,* 543 U.S. 1081 (2005). In 1977, Florida enacted a statute that made it patently illegal for gay people to adopt, regardless of the best interests of the child. FLA. STAT. ANN. § 63.042(3) (West 2005). The statute was challenged and upheld by the Eleventh Circuit in *Lofton. Lofton,* 358 F.3d at 806. In that case, the Eleventh Circuit considered evidence of discriminatory intent in the passage of the bill, including homophobic remarks by representatives discussing the legislation. *Id.* at 826–27. Nonetheless, the court reasoned that as long as there was any conceivably rational purpose underlying the statute, the court had to uphold it. *Id.* at 818. The statute was subsequently invalidated by *In re* Adoption of Doe. *In re* Adoption of Doe, 2008 WL 5006172, *29 (Fla. Cir. Ct. Nov. 25, 2008). The statute was still not repealed until July 1, 2015, though by then it had not been enforced in five years. Gary Fineout, *Florida Legislature Repeals State Ban on Gay Adoption,* AP NEWS (April 14, 2015), [https://perma.cc/E7KT-4U43].

[54] *Morrissey,* 871 F.3d at 1268.

[55] *In re Adoption of Doe,* 2008 WL 5070056, at *10 (Fla. Cir. Ct. Aug. 29, 2008) (quoting *Gay Bills Pass Both Chambers,* FLA. TIMES-UNION (June 1, 1977)).

justification for action against that group even under rational basis review.[56]

Of course, in our case we had argued that family formation deserves heightened scrutiny as a fundamental right and cited to the landmark case of *Skinner v. Oklahoma*.[57] In *Skinner*, the Court announced that procreation was indeed "fundamental to the very existence and survival of the [human] race" and is a "basic civil right[ ] of man."[58]

In applying *Skinner* to my case, the court decided that the right we were asserting was not a broad fundamental right to procreate, but instead a narrow right to an IRS deduction related to a specific and novel kind of procreation through IVF and surrogacy.[59] Describing my situation in that way made the general right to procreation inapplicable in our case.

The conclusion that we had no fundamental right to procreation through IVF and surrogacy, of course, once again ignores that fact that IVF and surrogacy in our case were the only route to procreation. Therefore, my very ability to procreate generally was at stake. Any government treatment of that fundamental right that is restrictive should,

---

56 Romer v. Evans, 517 U.S. 620, 631–36 (1996).

57 Skinner v. Oklahoma *ex rel.* Williamson, 316 U.S. 535 (1942).

58 *Id.* at 541.

59 *Morrissey*, 871 F.3d at 1269–70.

therefore, receive heightened scrutiny. And so, we appealed.

In August of 2017, the oral arguments for my case against the IRS were presented to the Eleventh Circuit Federal Court of Appeals in Montgomery, Alabama.[60] I wandered around Montgomery the afternoon before our oral arguments were to take place and was moved when I visited the Civil Rights Memorial Center and the Rosa Parks Museum. Etched into the wall in front of the Civil Rights Memorial Center, just above the memorial fountain, that has water spilling over its edges, are Martin Luther King, Jr.'s words (quoting from the Bible): ". . . until justice rolls down like waters, and righteousness like a mighty stream."[61]

Even though tax deductions cannot approach horrors like the lynchings that are remembered at the Civil Rights Memorial Center, the memorial also reminds visitors of Robert Kennedy's speech in South Africa in 1966 when he said, "[f]ew will have the greatness to bend history; but each of us can work to change a small portion of the events, and in the total of all these acts will be written the history of this generation."[62] And so, we marched into the imposing federal courthouse on that sweaty August day in Montgomery, cautious but somehow optimistic.

---

60 *Id.* at 1272, *aff'g* 226 F. Supp. 3d 1338 (M.D. Fla. 2016).

61 Dr. Martin Luther King, Jr. spoke those words during his famous "I Have a Dream" speech. Martin Luther King, Jr., I Have a Dream (Aug. 28, 1963).

62 Robert F. Kennedy, Day of Affirmation Address at the University of Capetown (June 6, 1966).

As I mentioned at the outset of this chapter, we lost. The appellate court agreed with the IRS that the relevant statute categorized our medical expenses as unnecessary and therefore any deduction was unavailable.[63]

While the results in our case were upsetting, losing our case at the Eleventh Circuit was hardly surprising. The Eleventh Circuit is the same circuit that upheld Florida's outright ban on gay people adopting in *Lofton* in 2004.[64]

It was, however, disheartening to receive subsequent advice from the law firm representing us that we should not proceed to challenge the ruling in the United States Supreme Court. Their opinion was corroborated by highly accomplished, nationally

---

[63] *See* Morrissey, *supra* note 23, at 368 n. 11 (explaining the history of Florida's anti-gay adoption laws at the statutory level and in the courts).

[64] Lofton v. Sec'y of the Dep't of Children & Family Servs., 358 F.3d 804, 806 (11th Cir. 2004), *cert. denied*, 543 U.S. 1081 (2005). In 1977, Florida enacted a statute that made it patently illegal for gay people to adopt, regardless of the best interests of the child. FLA. STAT. ANN. § 63.042(3) (West 2005). The statute was challenged and upheld by the Eleventh Circuit in *Lofton*. *Lofton*, 358 F.3d at 806. In that case, the Eleventh Circuit considered evidence of discriminatory intent in the passage of the bill, including homophobic remarks by representatives discussing the legislation. *Id.* at 826–27. Nonetheless, the court reasoned that as long as there was any conceivably rational purpose underlying the statute, the court had to uphold it. *Id.* at 818. The statute was subsequently invalidated by *In re* Adoption of Doe. *In re* Adoption of Doe, 2008 WL 5006172, *29 (Fla. Cir. Ct. Nov. 25, 2008). The statute was still not repealed until July 1, 2015, though by then it had not been enforced in five years. Gary Fineout, *Florida Legislature Repeals State Ban on Gay Adoption*, AP NEWS (April 14, 2015), [https://perma.cc/E7KT-4U43].

known civil rights attorneys. Given the increasingly conservative composition of the Supreme Court by 2017, we were told that the Court was unlikely to vindicate civil rights of any sort, and might, in fact, use the case as an opportunity to set back the civil rights gains made on behalf of gay people in recent decades.

As disheartening as it was to lose our case in the federal courts, I was reminded by civil rights advocates that it takes a sea of struggles and a mountain of losses before fundamental and equal rights are vindicated. They told me that each loss is one step further on the road to vindicate those rights. Hopefully, our case will provide some support for the next case or legislative initiative, when those rights are vindicated, making family formation more feasible for more people.

# CHAPTER 11

# INSURANCE

Another crucial piece of the surrogacy arrangement is insurance. Intended parents are typically expected to cover any medical expenses that will be incurred along the way. Insurance is crucial to making sure that these costs are covered.

If intended parents are working with an agency, the agency itself may mandate insurance coverage for the surrogate. Regardless of whether an agency is involved, having insurance is the only way to make sure that medical costs are predictable and manageable. Trying to pay those expenses out of pocket could result in a disaster if there is a medical emergency and then suddenly the medical bills amount to hundreds of thousands of dollars.

So, having insurance to cover as much of the medical expenses related to the surrogacy arrangement is vital, but it is also complicated. Don't make the mistake of thinking just because you or the surrogate have health insurance, that the medical expenses related to the surrogacy will be covered. Many insurance policies have specific exceptions in them stating that any surrogacy related medical expenses are specifically not covered.

This chapter will give you an overview of how intended parents should manage insurance coverage to make sure that insurance helps you manage surrogacy related medical expenses. It's easiest to think about surrogacy related medical expenses in three phases. Those three phases correspond to the timeline of a surrogacy arrangement: (i) first, are the expenses incurred pre-pregnancy, including fertility treatments and any sperm or egg donations, (ii) second, are expenses related to the pregnancy, and (iii) third, are medical expenses for any resulting children once they are born.

In addition to insurance covering these medical expenses, it is also typical and appropriate for the intended parents to purchase a life insurance policy to cover the surrogate. That policy ensures that the surrogate's dependents would receive a significant financial death benefit in the unlikely event of her death.

**Insurance Needs**

Costs involved in surrogacy are considerable. To make sure that they are predictable and manageable, intended parents should make sure that there is insurance in place, to the extent possible, to cover:

(i) Medical expenses incurred ***pre-pregnancy***, including fertility treatments and any sperm or egg donations;

(ii) Medical expenses related to the surrogate's ***pregnancy***;

(iii) Medical expenses related to any ***resulting child or children*** once they are born; and

(iv) ***Life insurance*** covering the life of the surrogate.

## 1. PRE-PREGNANCY MEDICAL EXPENSES

For each of the three medical phases of a surrogacy arrangement, intended parents will want to figure out whether any existing insurance coverage will apply to the expenses that are likely to be incurred. In this pre-pregnancy phase, costs are likely to be associated with fertility diagnoses and treatments, medications, IVF, pre-implantation genetic testing, and embryo transfers.

In addition, if any sperm or egg donation is necessary there will be associated costs. While sperm donations are not risky or particularly costly, egg donations are both. An egg donor will undergo significant and costly medical procedures, including taking a variety of expensive medications. Egg donors are also at risk for potential medical complications that could even be life threatening. Intended parents will want to be especially sure that any of those potentially extraordinary costs will be covered.

With all of these pre-pregnancy related expenses, some health insurance policies will cover certain costs, but some will not. Intended parents should be sure to call their insurance carrier and find out what exactly will be covered and what won't be. To the extent that existing insurance coverage does not cover expected costs, a specific insurance policy should be purchased that will cover those expenses.

Some states actually regulate insurance for infertility costs.[1] As of 2022, almost half of the states, twenty, have some sort of fertility coverage law. In addition to that, fourteen mandate coverage for IVF in certain circumstances. The twenty states that regulate insurance for fertility issues include: Arkansas, California, Colorado, Connecticut, Delaware, Hawaii, Illinois, Louisiana, Maine, Maryland, Massachusetts, Montana, New Hampshire, New Jersey, New York, Ohio, Rhode Island, Texas, Utah, and West Virginia.

But, again, take nothing for granted. Even in a state with infertility insurance laws, some policies may not be required to provide insurance for infertility issues. Intended parents should be sure to contact their insurance provider and ask all the questions about what specifically will be covered in their situation.

Questions to ask begin with whether doctors' appointments will be covered for infertility related concerns, including a diagnosis of infertility. You will also want to know then if fertility treatments would be covered, including fertility medications, and IVF procedures. Will an embryo transfer be covered? What about pre-implantation genetic testing?

You may find that you are covered, especially if you are an intended parent who will be using her own

---

[1] See the National Infertility Association's webpage, *Insurance Coverage by State*, RESOLVE, https://resolve.org/learn/financial-resources-for-family-building/insurance-coverage/insurance-coverage-by-state/ (last visited July 1, 2023), for a detailed discussion of insurance laws related to fertility.

eggs in a surrogacy arrangement. If, however, you are going to need to use an egg donor, the chances of the donor's expenses being covered are low. You'll want to ask those specific questions to your insurance carrier as well. What if we need an egg donor—will associated medical costs be covered?

There are policies that can cover certain medical expenses associated with egg donations. If you are working with an agency, your agency may have some advice for you in procuring the appropriate insurance. In fact, your agency may require that you procure that insurance.

There are at least a few insurance companies that specialize in finding health insurance coverage for all aspects of a surrogate arrangement, including egg donor medical expenses. One of those companies is ART Risk.[2] The other is International Fertility Insurance.[3] I have never worked with either of those companies and so cannot make any specific recommendation about either of them. I encourage any intended parent who needs insurance to consider those or any other company that might help you find the insurance you need.

Because insurance can also be costly, you may be tempted to manage some costs out-of-pocket and not bother with insurance. That is extremely risky. Insurance exists to help individuals manage risk.

---

[2] *ART Risk Fin. & Ins. Sol.*, https://artrisksolutions.com (last visited July 1, 2023).

[3] *Int'l Fertility Ins.*, https://www.internationalfertilityinsurance.com (last visited July 1, 2023).

With each aspect of surrogacy, including egg donation, there is always a risk of medical complications. Expenses associated with those complications can be astronomical. Insurance makes sure that you are not caught in a situation that is simply financially unmanageable.

**Insurance Versus Paying out of Pocket**

Because insurance itself can be costly, intended parents might be tempted to manage costs out of pocket. Beware! You might be able to estimate and manage costs associated with surrogacy when everything goes perfectly. But costs associated with any medical complications can be astronomical. Insurance helps you limit that risk and make sure those costs are manageable.

## 2. PREGNANCY RELATED MEDICAL EXPENSES

In a surrogacy arrangement, it is the surrogate who needs to be covered by insurance for all her pregnancy related medical needs. It is possible that the surrogate's own health insurance policy would cover her pregnancy related expenses. However, intended parents should be sure to contact the surrogate's insurance carrier and make sure that she would be covered. Because of privacy concerns, the surrogate may need to facilitate that contact. Alternatively, an agency might have insurance experts involved to assess the surrogate's own health insurance policy and find out what it covers. Many health insurance policies have a carve out for surrogacy, meaning they don't cover any pregnancy related expenses when the insured is acting as a surrogate.

| **Be Proactive in Communicating with Insurers** |
|---|
| It is crucial to communicate with insurance companies in advance to ensure coverage so that there are no surprises after expenses are incurred. Some health insurance providers cover surrogacy related pregnancies and some do not. Even when procuring a secondary policy to specifically cover surrogacy pregnancies, be sure that the secondary policy works effectively with the primary policy and doesn't negate any benefits. |

If the surrogate's health insurance doesn't cover her when she is acting as a surrogate, then the intended parents will want to purchase a policy that will cover her. A surrogacy agency or your attorney may well be equipped to find that insurance for you, or at least assist you in the process. If not, you might need to find insurance coverage for the surrogate on your own.

Again, insurance companies like ART Risk[4] and International Fertility Insurance exist to help intended parents find the right coverage for their situation.[5] But again, I have never used those intermediaries, and encourage intended parents to

---

4 *ART Risk Fin. & Ins. Sol.*, *supra* note 2.

5 *Int'l Fertility Ins.*, *supra* note 3.

investigate their services before deciding whether and how to proceed.

Getting the appropriate coverage for your surrogate might be as simple as finding an appropriate Affordable Care Act (ACA) compliant policy for the surrogate during open enrollment. The Affordable Care Act is the federal law that was enacted in 2010 to make health insurance more affordable for more people. An ACA policy can make sure that your surrogate's pregnancy related medical expenses are covered and manageable. Intended parents will need to figure out when the open enrollment period is in their state and then decide whether procuring an ACA policy at that time makes sense in their circumstances.

If an ACA policy is not available for your needs or you are outside of the open enrollment period, then you may need to consider purchasing an insurance policy through an insurance dealer (like ART Risk or International Fertility Insurance). A dealer may end up routing you to purchase a policy provided by Lloyd's of London (Lloyd's). Lloyd's does provide surrogacy specific insurance to meet the needs of any particular case.

In some cases, you will need to purchase a policy that will be the surrogate's primary health care policy but also will cover her pregnancy related medical expenses while acting as a surrogate. In other cases, when the surrogate has a primary policy that excludes surrogacy expenses, then the policy you'll need to purchase will be a secondary policy to cover just the surrogacy related pregnancy expenses.

If there are going to be two policies, it is essential that intended parents make sure that the primary policy allows a secondary policy, and that the surrogate will not lose out on any of the benefits of her primary policy simply because a secondary policy was purchased. Once again, it is crucial to communicate with the insurance companies in advance to ensure coverage so that there are no surprises after expenses are incurred.

**Tales from the Field: Insurance Expired**

In one recent surrogacy arrangement, the intended parents met their surrogate with the help of a surrogacy agency. With the agency's guidance, the parties did their appropriate insurance homework before they embarked on their arrangement. To their delight, the intended parents found that the surrogate's own primary health insurance, which she obtained through her employment, actually did cover surrogacy related medical expenses. The intended parents were thrilled not to have to pay for any additional or supplemental insurance policy to ensure medical coverage for the pregnancy.

Unfortunately, early into the pregnancy and with income from the surrogacy coming in, the surrogate decided to quit her job. Accordingly, her insurance, which she obtained through her job, also lapsed. The surrogate did inform the surrogacy agency about this development. The agency should have been proactive and counseled the parties to either have the surrogate to make continuing payments to extend her existing insurance coverage or to purchase a new policy.

Unfortunately, the agency somehow did not take any action. Instead, the intended parents learned about the lapse in insurance coverage later on in the pregnancy when they received unexpectedly large bills in connection with the surrogate's medical care.

The intended parents contacted their surrogacy agency. Luckily for the intended parents, the surrogacy agency took responsibility for not contacting the intended parents about the lapse in the insurance policy. The surrogacy agency paid the extra expenses and procured insurance to cover the rest of the pregnancy.

As that tale from the field illustrates, even understanding what the insurance situation is at the outset of a relationship with a surrogate does not guaranty that the situation won't change. If the intended parents are going to be relying on the surrogate's health insurance to cover medical costs, the intended parents will want to get a commitment from the surrogate that she will inform them if circumstances change and not hold them responsible if she doesn't. Clear, effective, and regular communications between the intended parents and the surrogate are, once again, paramount.

### 3. POST BIRTH MEDICAL EXPENSES

This phase is typically the easiest in terms of insurance. In a surrogacy arrangement, once one or more children are born and the intended parent or parents are declared the parent, that intended parent's own health insurance should cover any medical expenses the child or children incur. Once again, however, every intended parent should contact their insurance carrier and make sure this is the case.

It is also prudent for any intended parent to notify their health insurance carrier in any event, once their surrogate is pregnant, so that the insurance company is ready to cover the child or children once they are born. The hospital or other medical facility where the surrogate will deliver will also want to know in advance which insurance policy will be covering the medical expenses of any children born. That is also true for any medical providers, including the doctors who will be attending the child or children once they are born.

## 4. SURROGATE LIFE INSURANCE

We've just reviewed how insurance can be essential to managing costs associated with a surrogacy arrangement, from the pre-pregnancy expenses, through pregnancy, and then after childbirth. But another important piece to the surrogate's insurance coverage is life insurance.

Again, insurance exists to manage risk. While the risk is low, there is always some small chance that some extraordinary and tragic medical emergency will arise and the surrogate may lose her life. Life insurance covering the surrogate will make sure that her family will get some significant death benefit to help them as they deal with their loss and attempt to move forward.

Once again, this insurance policy would be paid for by the intended parents. It may even be mandated by the relevant surrogacy agency, or required by the surrogate pursuant to the surrogacy agreement. Insurance companies like ART Risk or International Fertility Insurance can help intended parents find the right coverage. Agencies and family formation lawyers are also likely to have good recommendations.

Insurance is all about managing risk. Surrogacy involves a significant amount of risk. From the pre-pregnancy stage up through the birth of the children, egg donors and surrogates in particular are taking on significant health risks by agreeing to help intended parents. While the health concerns themselves can't be mitigated completely, the financial aspects of those risks can and should be managed with the right insurance.

# CHAPTER 12
# INTERNATIONALIZATION

More and more, people are looking globally for medical help, services, and procedures. For intended parents from countries where surrogacy is illegal, international surrogacy is the only legally available option. Those intended parents can proceed in a relatively secure legal environment if they choose to proceed in a country like the United States. The United States is in fact increasingly an international surrogacy destination, chosen for its generally reliable legal regulatory regime; helpful and established surrogacy agencies; availability of well-educated, responsible egg donors and surrogates; and sophisticated medical system.

But some intended parents in the United States have worked with agencies outside of the United States to find an egg donor and a surrogate. Indeed, more and more intended parents from the United States are choosing to proceed outside of the United States because of the affordability of surrogacy in other jurisdictions.

## 1. INCREASED RISKS

However, there are increased risks involved with any intended parents attempting surrogacy in a foreign jurisdiction. For intended parents from the United States, surrogacy may well cost far less in a foreign country than it does in the United States. However, there are complications that can arise from unclear foreign regulatory systems, changing foreign laws and rules, establishing parental rights, and getting the necessary government approvals to leave the foreign country with the child or children.

In many foreign countries there are also informal customs for getting things done that involve facilitation payments made to the right people. And if there are medical complications with the pregnancy or birth, the intended parents might find themselves spending more time in the foreign jurisdiction and being more reliant on their overall health care system than they initially thought. In those cases, it is crucial that the local health care system is sophisticated enough to manage those health complications.

And disputes are always possible in complex legal arrangements. With surrogacy, disputes tend to revolve around custody and parental rights, but those disputes might involve money paid or owed to the surrogate, the egg donor, or the local agency. Disputes also could arise over negligent medical care or other issues. If there are any disputes, they will likely need to be resolved in the courts of the foreign jurisdiction and possibly in a foreign language. For intended parents from the United States proceeding abroad, that means hiring a local lawyer and somehow managing the dispute resolution from a distance or traveling frequently to that foreign location.

In the end, any international legal dispute is likely to be costly and complicated, potentially eclipsing any cost savings associated with the surrogacy arrangement itself. Any intended parent considering international surrogacy should consult with the local agency on how dispute resolution would proceed. If the answer is that disputes would be resolved in the local courts, then the intended parents need to be comfortable with the idea that they may need to hire local lawyers to represent their interests in those court proceedings.

**International Surrogacy Risks**

While proceeding with surrogacy outside of the United States may well be more affordable generally, it also comes with a variety of increased risks, including:

(i) whether the foreign jurisdiction has laws that allow surrogacy for the intended parents pursuing it (including single intended parents and/or gay intended parents);

(ii) whether the foreign jurisdiction has a history of changing its legal regulations, making it risky even if surrogacy is legally allowed in that jurisdiction at the planning stage;

(iii) whether the health care system in the foreign jurisdiction is sufficiently sophisticated to manage potential health complications;

(iv) what bureaucratic and legal hurdles will need to be managed to establish parental rights in the foreign jurisdiction and get passports to return home; and

(v) any legal disputes that do arise may need to be resolved in the local courts of the foreign jurisdiction.

Intended parents from the United States, where surrogacy is now legal and supported in the majority of the states, should think through all of the additional risks that are associated with proceeding internationally with surrogacy. Those added risks need to be weighed against the benefit of lower costs. Some case studies are helpful to illustrate what can happen with international surrogacy arrangements—some have been successful, and some have been a nightmare.

## 2. TALES FROM THE FIELD: FROM SAN FRANCISCO TO INDIA . . . AND BACK

One same-sex married couple I spoke with live in San Francisco. They had spoken to each other about wanting children on their very first date. By 2010 they were seriously pursuing forming a family via surrogacy.

They started by speaking with representatives from a popular California surrogacy agency, but did not get a good first impression. To them, the agency representative seemed to stress aspects of family formation that seemed superficial, focusing on creating children with the right skin, hair and eye color, rather than having healthy children who would have a supportive and loving home. Moreover, the costs that were being discussed seemed extremely high.

This couple then found a lawyer in the Berkeley area who ran an agency. The couple loved everything about her and how she ran her agency. She did seem to focus on all the right issues for this couple.

Unfortunately, as the couple were in discussions with her, she shifted her business focus to strictly provide the legal support for surrogacy.

Then this couple heard about surrogacy in India. One of the men had worked in India extensively and was very comfortable with the idea of proceeding there. The medical system was well regarded, and surrogacy was far more affordable.

Commercial surrogacy (meaning surrogates being paid for their services) was legalized in India in 2002.[1] With a large number of women willing to act as surrogates for relatively high pay, India developed as a hub of surrogacy.[2] Intended parents from the United States could expect high quality care for roughly one-third the price they would end up paying in the United States. One well known agency back in 2013 would charge foreign couples $25,000 to $30,000 and that would include all the surrogacy fees, agency fees, and medical fees.

The Indian surrogates themselves would earn roughly $6,500—an enormous amount by local

---

1 Nita Bhalla & Mansi Thapliyal, *India Seeks to Regulate Its Booming 'Rent-a-Womb' Industry*, REUTERS (Sept. 30, 2013, 4:31 AM), https://www.reuters.com/article/us-india-surrogates/india-seeks-to-regulate-its-booming-rent-a-womb-industry-idUSBRE98T07F20130930.

2 *See* Eshan Sonak & Sanvi Bhatia, *India's New Surrogacy Regulation Bill Falls Short of Protecting Bodily Autonomy and Guaranteeing Reproductive Liberty*, LONDON SCH. OF ECON. & POL. SCI.: LSE HUM. RTS. (Apr. 21, 2021), https://blogs.lse.ac.uk/humanrights/2021/04/21/indias-new-surrogacy-regulation-bill-falls-short-of-protecting-bodily-autonomy-and-guaranteeing-reproductive-liberty/.

standards—many multiples of a typical annual salary for many women.[3] So, the financial incentive for being a surrogate was huge for these women. Those earnings could change their lives and potentially the lives of their families.

By 2012, the value of the surrogacy market in India was estimated by a United Nations backed study to be roughly $400 million dollars per year.[4] Thousands of fertility clinics were operating throughout the country.[5]

The intended parents in this case did an internet search for surrogacy agencies in India and found one whose web presence they liked. After discussions with agency representatives online and on the phone, the couple decided to embark on a true journey—a journey to India to meet with this surrogacy agency located in New Delhi.

What they learned was that with this agency, and most of the surrogacy agencies in India, the surrogates come to live together in a community house with great medical care immediately available and an in-house chef who served nutritious meals. Egg donors were also available and were strictly vetted for a healthy background. Both surrogates' and egg donors' identities would be kept anonymous. So, there would be no direct contact between either the surrogate or the donor and the intended parents. However, the agency would send the intended

---

[3] Bhalla & Thapliyal, *supra* note 1.

[4] *Id.*

[5] *Id.*

parents weekly reports and updates on their surrogacy process.

Once a surrogate became pregnant, there would also be regular ultrasound procedures with the images sent to the intended parents. Pretty quickly into the pregnancy, the ultrasound procedures were done weekly to assure healthy fetal development.

This couple really liked what they learned, what they saw, and how they felt when meeting with the agency representatives in India. And so, like all intended parents pursuing surrogacy, this couple decided to take the plunge, manage the risks of surrogacy the best that they could, and move forward. They left a sperm donation and a financial deposit and went back to the United States hopeful that they would become pregnant soon.

Amazingly, this couple actually decided to move forward with two surrogates, and have each receive two embryos that were fertilized by a different one of the intended dads. Their hope was that they might end up with two children, with each one being genetically linked to a different one of the intended dads. Of course, they recognized that they might have ended up with two, three, or even four or more children. Still, they were prepared, and even excited, about the possibility of having an instantly large family.

The result of that round of embryo transfers for this couple was one successful pregnancy. Their first child was born in New Delhi with no complications whatsoever. They coordinated the necessary approvals and paperwork to establish parenthood and be allowed to leave the country with their daughter.

The hurdles of establishing parenthood and getting the approvals to leave the country were significant. They were assisted by their local Indian lawyers and managed to navigate the process fairly easily, despite the process being nerve wracking.

An exit visa had to be procured by first working with the Indian Ministry of Home Affairs (MHA). Documents establishing parenthood had to be filed with the MHA. Then, documents from the MHA had to be delivered to the Foreign Regional Registration Office for the intended parents to finally be cleared from the Indian government side to leave India with their daughter. But the couple also had to get a United States passport for their daughter, and that meant more paperwork and a visit to the United States Embassy.

With all the necessary approvals and documents in hand, about ten days after the birth of their daughter, the couple flew back to the United States from India together with their newborn. Within a few weeks, they were back in San Francisco as a family of three.

But the story doesn't end there. Encouraged by their success and the relative ease of their surrogacy experience with their first daughter, the couple immediately went into a contract with their surrogacy agency to go through surrogacy again. This time, with one daughter already a part of the family, they decided to contract with only one surrogate and use the sperm of the intended father who was not the genetically related dad of their first daughter.

It's the rare journey that doesn't have any road bumps. Within a short time after agreeing to pursue surrogacy in India for a second time, India issued new rules banning surrogacy for foreign gay couples or single people.[6] Those new rules categorically precluded this gay couple from the United States from being able to proceed in India.

But—luckily for the intended parents—there was an exception. Any intended parents who were already under contract for surrogacy were allowed to continue with the process. And so, it happened for this couple again.

The clinic transferred two embryos into the surrogate and the couple ended up with two beautiful children as a result of that process. The couple travelled back to India again after their twins were born. They again coordinated all the paperwork to establish parenthood and be allowed to leave the country with their newborn twins. Finally, they arrived back home in San Francisco as a family of five.

Looking back on the experience over ten years later, the dads are thrilled with their beautiful and healthy family. The children are thriving back in San

---

6 *India Bans Gay Foreign Couples from Surrogacy*, THE TEL. (Jan. 18, 2013, 2:57 PM), https://www.telegraph.co.uk/news/worldnews/asia/india/9811222/India-bans-gay-foreign-couples-from-surrogacy.html.

Francisco. But the dad I spoke to acknowledged all of the complexities and risks of their surrogacy journey in India. "The lack of information we had going into it was astounding . . . we made our decisions by gut and faith, and somehow it all worked out."

International surrogacy arrangements, like all international arrangements, come with the added complexity of navigating the foreign jurisdiction, including the laws and regulations of that jurisdiction. The case just discussed is a great example of this. The couple from California ran into changing foreign rules that might have prohibited them from proceeding with their second surrogacy arrangement—or worse—might have prevented them from actually gaining custody of their children if their children had already been born in India when the local rules changed.

Had a dispute over parental rights arisen in this case after the surrogate had gotten pregnant, the intended parents would likely have found themselves thrust into the Indian court system. As we will see in other case studies below, resolution of these cases is not often quick and is also not always in the intended parents' favor.

Surrogacy continues to be controversial globally. There have been reports, in India and elsewhere, of surrogates being exploited.[7] The potential for exploitation and resulting commodification of the

---

[7] Bhalla & Thapliyal, *supra* note 1.

women who agree to be surrogates has been one of the primary criticisms of surrogacy in general.

Empirical research has shown that exploitation has not typically been found in surrogacy relationships in developed markets like the United States. However, exploitation is more likely in lesser developed countries, where the compensation for the surrogate is so lucrative that the women are lured into strictly controlled arrangements that might not be healthy for them.[8] Women in those arrangements may even give up control over medical decisions affecting their own bodies. Some of those decisions include whether and when to terminate a pregnancy or whether to proceed with a pregnancy even if it would be life threatening for the surrogate. Prohibiting, limiting, or regulating surrogacy is often discussed as a way to protect these women from being exploited.

But there are other interests that jurisdictions weigh in the balance, the reproductive freedom of the surrogate to proceed as she sees fit while earning compensation that could change her life. And, of course, there are the interests of the intended parents in being able to form biologically related families.

[8] Sara L. Ainsworth, *Bearing Children, Bearing Risks: Feminist Leadership for Progressive Regulation of Compensated Surrogacy in the United States*, 89 WASH. L. REV. 1077, 1088 (2014).

**Regulatory Balancing Acts**

As in the United States, critics and regulators around the globe have had to balance concerns when arriving at a regulatory regime for surrogacy. On the one hand, there are concerns that surrogacy can involve the exploitation and commodification of the women involved acting as either egg donors or surrogates. On the other hand, there are the liberty interests of the women who want to be involved having the freedom to do so. On that side of the scale, there are also the interests of the intended parents in having biologically related children.

Exploitation is even more of a concern in developing countries where surrogate compensation is extraordinarily high relative to average local salaries. That high surrogate compensation can essentially coerce young women into agreeing to very strict arrangements that may not be in their best interests.

Inside the United States, the majority of states now permit commercial surrogacy, although they also regulate it. Outside of the United States, many advanced and developing nations have balanced the concerns and decided to categorically prohibit commercial surrogacy.

India has struggled with balancing those competing interests, and in 2022 India amended its surrogacy law again. Commercial surrogacy is now entirely banned in India.[9] Only altruistic (unpaid) surrogacy is permitted and only for married Indian couples with a variety of additional requirements for both intended parents and surrogates.[10] Accordingly, India is no longer a legally viable option for any intended parent from the United States.

Many other countries also currently either prohibit commercial surrogacy altogether or prohibit it for foreign intended parents. Those countries include: Austria, Australia, Belgium, Brazil, Canada, China, Estonia, France, Germany, Italy, Lithuania, Malaysia, Nepal, the Netherlands, New Zealand, Norway, Poland, Russia, Spain, Sweden, Switzerland, Thailand, and the United Kingdom.

As we have discussed many of the states in the United States now do permit commercial surrogacy and enforce surrogacy agreements. Other countries where commercial surrogacy is currently either expressly permitted, or otherwise generally practiced include: Albania, Armenia, Colombia, Cyprus, Georgia, Guatemala, Kenya, Mexico (be aware of United States State Department warning, discussed below), and Ukraine.

But before deciding on international surrogacy, a few other cases are worth considering to more fully appreciate the risks. One of those cases is the case of

---

[9] *See Nayanthara-Vignesh Controversy: What Laws Regulate Surrogacy in India*, THE INDIAN EXPRESS (Oct. 13, 2022, 3:43 PM), https://indianexpress.com/article/explained/what-laws-regulate-surrogacy-in-india-nayanthara-vignesh-8202717/, for an overview of surrogacy laws in India.

[10] *Id.*

Baby Manji Yamata, a case that again involved surrogacy in India.[11] The other case is the case of Baby Boy Daneth, born to a surrogate in Cambodia.

## 3. TALES FROM THE FIELD: THE INDIAN CASE STUDY OF *BABY MANJI YAMATA*[12]

In the case of Baby Manji Yamata, the intended parents were Japanese, and the surrogacy arrangement was made with a surrogate in Gujarat, India. The intended father was Dr. Yuki Yamada and the intended mother was his wife, Dr. Ikufumi Yamata. The surrogacy contract was signed in 2007 and Baby Manji Yamata was born in July of 2008.

While the surrogate was pregnant with their child, the intended parents divorced. The intended father still wanted to establish parenthood of the child born and take custody, but the intended mother did not. Indian laws prohibited single men from adopting. Consequently, the intended father was precluded from legally becoming the child's parent in India. Moreover, he could not get the travel documents needed to take the child out of the country.

The case ended up going from the Rajasthani courts all the way up to the Supreme Court of India.[13] After much time, heartache, effort, and money spent,

---

[11] Marcy Darnovsky, *Complications of Surrogacy: The Case of Baby Manji*, CTR. FOR GENETICS AND SOC'Y: BIOPOLITICAL TIMES (Sept. 18, 2009), https://www.geneticsandsociety.org/biopolitical-times/complications-surrogacy-case-baby-manji.

[12] Baby Manji Yamada v. Union of India & Anr. (2008) 13 SCC 518 (India), https://indiankanoon.org/doc/854968/.

[13] *Id.*

the intended father was finally and ultimately allowed custody of Baby Manji.[14]

## 4. TALES FROM THE FIELD: THE CAMBODIAN CASE STUDY OF *BABY BOY DANETH*[15]

This nightmare began when Xu Wenjun, a Chinese businessman from Hong Kong, embarked on a surrogacy journey as an intended father with a surrogacy agency in Cambodia. Xu was matched with a local Cambodian surrogate, a young married woman named Hun Daneth. Hun became pregnant with Xu's child in 2017 when suddenly Cambodia began to enforce a ban on commercial surrogacy.

Prior to 2017, commercial surrogacy had been thriving in Cambodia after other Asian countries, like India, enacted restrictions or strict prohibitions on the arrangement. Then, in 2016, the Ministry of Health in Cambodia announced a ban on surrogacy. Still, though, Cambodia never actually followed through to enact any legislation prohibiting surrogacy. And so, surrogacy in Cambodia continued.

In 2017 Cambodian authorities began to use existing laws prohibiting human trafficking to arrest surrogates on the grounds that the babies they were having would be sold to third parties, effectively

---

14 *Id.*

15 *See* Hannah Beech, *They Were Surrogates. Now They Must Raise the Children*, N.Y. TIMES, https://www.nytimes.com/2022/11/26/world/asia/surrogacy-cambodia.html?smid=em-share (last updated Dec. 14, 2022), for a detailed discussion of this case.

trafficked. Human trafficking was punishable by up to twenty years in prison.

Many surrogates who were pregnant at the time, including Hun, were imprisoned in a military hospital. Most had their babies while in custody, some chained to their delivery beds. Later, the women were sentenced to prison terms with the condition that they would be released immediately if they agreed to keep and raise the babies they had birthed for intended parents. In the event that any of the surrogates were found to have given up custody of the child born, they would be taken back into custody.

In the case of Baby Boy Daneth, Hun and her husband are now raising the child as their own. They are following the instructions from the judge who sentenced Hun. But they have grown attached and currently do not want to give up the boy.

The intended father, Xu, however, ended up in a Cambodian jail. He went to Cambodia himself in an attempt to bring his son home to China. He found Hun, visited his son and brought his son presents. He established that he was genetically the baby's father through paternity testing, and was able to secure a Chinese passport for the boy from the Chinese embassy. Nonetheless, while in Cambodia in 2020, Xu was arrested and sentenced to 15 years in prison for human trafficking. As of January 2023, Xu remains in prison with an appeal in the summer of 2022 being unsuccessful.

As we have seen generally, surrogacy involves managing a certain amount of risk. However, as these tales from the international field illustrate, international surrogacy is fraught with additional risks. Intended parents need to understand the legal regulations on surrogacy in the foreign jurisdiction. Moreover, those regulations may well change. Even if the regulations themselves don't change, enforcement policies may change. Any dispute may result in the intended parents facing the daunting prospect of navigating the local legal system and potentially even defending themselves in a criminal prosecution.

Navigating foreign jurisdictions even when there are no conflicts with local laws, regulations or any formal disputes, also means managing the surrogacy process from a distance for much of the time. It will also mean travelling to the foreign jurisdiction from time to time, as needed. Travelling to the local jurisdiction to take custody of the child or children born will be essential. At that stage, intended parents for sure will need to manage the local legal and bureaucratic hurdles to establish parental rights and be allowed to leave that country with their newborn child or children.

## 5. TALES FROM THE FIELD: SURROGACY IN MEXICO

With commercial surrogacy for foreign intended parents now largely illegal in Asia, many United States intended parents are turning to Mexico. The same concerns just mentioned as generally relevant for international surrogacy—concern over foreign legal regulations, changing laws or enforcement, access to quality health care, navigating local bureaucracy to establish parental rights, and facing the risk of dispute resolution in local courts—all also apply to surrogacy in Mexico for intended parents from the United States or any other country.

Despite the popularity of Mexico for intended parents from the United States, the United States State Department has actually issued a clear warning ***against*** proceeding with surrogacy in Mexico.

> Although surrogacy agencies/clinics claim surrogacy is legal in Mexico and actively promote Mexico as a destination for international commercial surrogacy, there is no legal framework for foreigners or same-sex couples to pursue surrogacy in Mexico. As a result, surrogacy agreements between foreign or same-sex intending parents and gestational mothers are not enforced by Mexican courts.[16]

Despite the risks, clearly outlined in the State Department's warning, intended parents continue to pursue commercial surrogacy in Mexico. I was in touch with one gay couple from the United States who had their child with a surrogate in Cancun, Mexico within the last year. They were generally

---

[16] U.S. Mission to Mex., *Surrogacy, ART and DNA Testing*, U.S. EMBASSY & CONSULATES IN MEX. (June 17, 2021), https://mx.usembassy.gov/surrogacy-art-and-dna-testing/.

impressed by the people at their agency and the health care services they received.

They thought that the entire process probably cost about half of what it might have in the United States. Still, they ended up needing to do several rounds of embryo transfers before getting pregnant. They paid over $100,000 when considering all of their expenses, including travel.

This couple did express frustration with having to manage the process from a distance. The intended father whom I spoke with said that their agency did make it clear that the legal aspects of establishing parental rights and getting a United States passport were the responsibility of the intended parents. The agency did provide some guidance on the process. Nonetheless, it took this couple three full and very stressful weeks in Mexico after their baby was born to complete the necessary bureaucratic hurdles to establish their parental rights, and then get a United States passport for their child so that they could return to the United States as a family.

For this couple, the process went about as smoothly as they expected. Thankfully for them, there were no surprises with changes of laws or enforcement. Further, this couple had no formal disputes with any of their Mexican counterparties that might have derailed the process and could have landed them in the Mexican court system. On balance, however, one of the intended fathers did say to me that if money wasn't a concern, they certainly would have proceeded locally in the United States.

As the world continues to become a smaller place, with international business and travel increasing all the time, it makes sense that even surrogacy would become an international phenomenon. For intended parents from jurisdictions where surrogacy is illegal, international surrogacy arrangements are likely the only legal option to having genetically related children. Those intended parents may well choose to proceed in a developed country like the United States where surrogacy is permitted, regulated, and supported by established agencies, available responsible surrogates and egg donors, and a sophisticated health care system.

For intended parents from the United States, international surrogacy abroad may be a more affordable option. In fact, for some, the cost savings may make the difference between being able to afford to proceed or not. However, the risks involved with international surrogacy arrangements in foreign countries, particularly lesser developed countries, should be considered and managed carefully. Foreign laws may not clearly permit surrogacy in any particular case. Sometimes surrogacy is permitted, but not for compensation, or perhaps not for single or gay intended parents. And, as we've seen from our case examples, laws and their enforcement can be subject to change. There are also bureaucratic hurdles involved with establishing parenthood and returning home that can make international surrogacy difficult. If there are any disputes, they may need to be resolved in local courts in the foreign jurisdiction, adding to costs and risks. In the end, each intended parent in the United States considering international surrogacy will need to weigh for themselves any potential cost savings against these increased risks.

# INDEX

**References are to Pages**